Praise for *The Daniel Dilemma*

"Like the prophet Daniel's beacon from Babylon, Chris Hodges offers us a wake-up call to shake off the cultural idolatry around us and instead stand firm in our faith. This book displays all the things I love about Chris—his honesty and humor, his practical approach and devotion to God's Word—this is his best yet!"

—CHRISTINE CAINE, founder of A21 and Propel Women

"*The Daniel Dilemma* inspires as it convicts, reminding us that the desperate, hurting people around us don't need to be proven wrong—they need Jesus. With tenderness and strength, compassion and clarity, Chris Hodges shows us how to be humble servants of God, just like the prophet Daniel, influencing our culture instead of being consumed by its humanistic hunger. This book is a field guide to living in our broken, twenty-first-century world today—a must-read!"

—JOHN C. MAXWELL, *New York Times* bestselling author, founder of John Maxwell Leadership Foundation

"This is one of the most needed messages of our time. Pastor Chris has wisely penned these words with solid truth and tender grace. He brings us back to what God's Word says regarding the cultural issues we're all wrestling with as Christians."

—LYSA TERKEURST, *New York Times* bestselling author, president of Proverbs 31 Ministries

"Significant. Timely. Relevant. Pastor Chris Hodges calls us to stand firmly on the Holy Ground found at the intersection of truth and love. Drawing from the example of one of the most beloved and stalwart men in Scripture, *The Daniel Dilemma* expounds on the believer's God-given responsibility to walk in grace and truth. I highly recommend this resource."

—LOUIE GIGLIO, pastor of Passion City Church, founder of Passion Conferences, author of *Goliath Must Fall*

"Chris honestly but gently teaches Christians to be bold, courageous, and godly examples of love in this dark and lost world. Grab this book and get ready to be inspired!"

—CRAIG GROESCHEL, *New York Times* bestselling author, pastor of Life.Church

"Using the life of Daniel as a blueprint, along with personal and engaging stories, Chris shows us how we can stand firm in our biblical beliefs while also loving people who are different from us."

—ROBERT MORRIS, founding senior pastor of Gateway Church, bestselling author of *The Blessed Life, The God I Never Knew, Truly Free,* and *Frequency*

"With one of the best explorations of Daniel I've ever seen, Chris Hodges illuminates our daily battle between God's light and culture's darkness. This book will convict you to stand stronger and inspire you to love more compassionately—in other words, to be more like Jesus!"

—TOMMY BARNETT, senior pastor of Dream City Church, cofounder of The Dream Center

"It isn't easy to be selfless in a selfie culture. If you've ever felt out of place in the world around you, then you need to read my friend's new book. Daniel didn't belong either, but he found a way to stand out for the right reasons. Pastor Chris Hodges shows us that we can do the same today, right where we are."

—GREG SURRATT, founding pastor of Seacoast Church, president of Association of Related Churches

"Chris Hodges offers an excellent guide to living a God-first life and makes it easy to understand the biblical principles by which we should live."

—PASTOR MATTHEW BARNETT, *New York Times* bestselling author, cofounder of The Dream Center

"I believe this book is a message desperately needed by our generation as we grapple to not put our convictions and love for others at odds."

—PASTOR RICH WILKERSON JR., lead pastor of VOUS Church

The Daniel Dilemma

How to Stand Firm and Love Well in a Culture of Compromise

Chris Hodges

NELSON BOOKS

An Imprint of Thomas Nelson

Published in Nashville, Tennessee, by Nelson Books, an imprint of Thomas Nelson. Nelson Books and Thomas Nelson are registered trademarks of HarperCollins Christian Publishing, Inc.

Published in association with Yates & Yates, www.yates2.com.

Thomas Nelson titles may be purchased in bulk for educational, business, fund-raising, or sales promotional use. For information, please e-mail SpecialMarkets@ThomasNelson.com.

ISBN 978-0-7180-9154-5 (eBook)

Library of Congress Control Number: 2017937423

ISBN 978-0-7180-9153-8 (TP)

Printed in the United States of America

17 18 19 20 21 LSC 10 9 8 7 6 5 4 3

To my children, Sarah, Michael, David, Jonathan, and Joseph.
You grew up in one of the most challenging cultures ever,
and like Daniel, you stood strong in your convictions while
loving everyone around you. When you were growing up, each
morning before you left for school, I told you to "be a leader,
not a follower." And now as adults you're doing just that. You
didn't let the world change you—you're changing the world!
I am so proud of you.

—DAD

CONTENTS

CONTENTS

Foreword

I am passionate about God's truth. I am also very compassionate with people. And sometimes those two dynamics can leave me wrestling. How do I stand firm on some of the harder scriptures while still loving people well? Is anyone doing this correctly?

Some charge head first and bowl people over with hard-hitting truths. Others swing the pendulum in the completely opposite direction by being so grace-filled they take on a liberal, rather than literal, interpretation of Scripture. And still others ignore the harder issues altogether.

But I don't want to do any of these things. I want to stand firm on God's Word and, at the same time, love people really well. That's why I'm so thankful that Chris has tackled this exact tension using the amazing examples we find in the life of Daniel.

Chris is completely committed to the purest and truest teaching of God's Word and, at the same time, to being absolutely lavish in his love for people. All people. I know you'll feel the tender compassion that's the truest reflection of Pastor Chris Hodges's heart as you read *The Daniel Dilemma*. That is why he's the perfect person to write this message. He gets the need to keep the words *grace* and *truth* together like harmonious notes of the most beautifully composed music.

Not only is this the way he teaches; this is the way he lives. I've seen it. But, even better, I've experienced it.

In one of the hardest moments of my life, I sat with Chris and his wife, Tammy. I had been hurt and wounded in a completely heart-shattering way. I wasn't just broken. I was shattered. I was a mess.

They were listening. I was sobbing. Life was crashing in on me, and my heart was imploding under the pressure. They tenderly guided me with truth and, at the same time, completely shepherded my heart with grace. There was no judgment. There was no assignment of fault or blame. There was no finger-pointing. There was nothing that added to my heartbreak.

There was truth. There was love. And at the intersection of that delicate balance there were Chris and Tammy with their arms wrapped around me.

It's been exactly one year since that day, and they are still both faithfully by my side. During this year, I've listened to almost every sermon Pastor Chris has loaded on the Church of the Highlands website, and I have learned so much from him. I love that he doesn't teach from the vantage point of his opinions—there's no need to when God has already given us his truth—but, rather, Chris keeps his heart in line with his own desperate need for God's truth and God's grace.

Just as he has walked with me, I believe he's the perfect guide to help you navigate the harder issues of today as well. Those issues that are deeply personal and affecting your own emotional and spiritual life in a very acute way right now. As well as those issues that are hard topics to tackle from a biblical standpoint.

Any time you are choosing a guide to get you through hard places, you want to know some very crucial things are true about them: that they are wise, that they are experienced, that they will care for you, and that they will get you through safely to the other side. All of this is true about Pastor Chris Hodges. I honestly can't think of a more qualified person to write this message. He knows it. He lives it. And he loves so very well through the process.

LYSA TERKEURST, *New York Times* bestselling author

Introduction ————————————————————————

Balancing Act—Standing Firm and Loving Well

Jesus Christ is the same yesterday and today and forever.

—HEBREWS 13:8

I t was one of the most unique gifts I'd ever received.
A friend in our church had blessed me for Christmas by giving me one of the most extravagant luxuries a man can have: a handmade, custom-tailored suit. I learned these suits are called "bespoke" by the British, who are famous for their Savile Row suit making, the height of high-end menswear. My appointment was with the best tailor in Birmingham, an older gentleman I'll call Joe. Born overseas, Joe had been tailoring in our country for decades, earning himself a national reputation for excellence.

When my wife, Tammy, and I arrived for my appointment—you didn't think I was going to pick out fabrics and buttons by myself, did you?—Joe greeted us at the entrance to his shop. It was a discreet, unadvertised location tucked in among dentists' offices and beauty parlors on the outskirts of downtown. The room he ushered us into smelled of starched linen and clean wool, and it was as neatly organized as the men's section at any department store. But mixed in among the fabric swatches and photos of garments on the walls, I noticed several tribal gods staring back at me.

"Welcome, Pastor and Mrs. Pastor!" said Joe, his eyes twinkling. "I am so happy to serve you today and will make you a beautiful suit for you to look your best!"

"It's going to take more than a new suit to help me look my best," I deadpanned as Joe chuckled and Tammy rolled her eyes. "But I hear you're the best in town, so if anyone can do it, you're the man!"

My appointment flew by as Joe measured and scribbled in his little notebook, recording more angles on my body than I knew existed. He patiently showed us flannels and tweeds, wool knits and synthetic blends of the finest fabrics from around the world. Who knew there were so many details in making a man's suit? Growing up, I just went to JCPenney like everyone else, and my mom bought a suit that was on sale and fit. Now, in Joe's capable hands, I looked like I was ready for *GQ*!

Finally, with our selections made, it was time to leave, and I thanked Joe sincerely for such a remarkable experience. "You are most welcome, Pastor," he said with a solemn smile. "You are a delight, not at all what I expected."

Curious, I said, "Why is that, Joe? What *did* you expect?"

He hesitated for a moment before saying, "I have made suits for many other pastors and people who tell me they are Christians. They see my people's gods on the wall and say they are not real. One man in particular [he named a nationally prominent leader known for evangelism] asked me to have a meal with him so he could tell me about your Jesus. I dined with him, but when I could not give him the answer he wanted, he told me I would be sent to hell." Joe's voice faltered with emotion. "You, on the other hand, seem most kind. You treat me with respect and make me laugh. I thank you. You are much different from what I was expecting."

"I'm sorry you have had such negative experiences with Christians," I said. "That is not the heart of Jesus. I'd love for you to meet the people I worship with so you can see it doesn't have to be that way. Would you be willing to visit my church?"

"Me? Visit your church?" he said, genuinely surprised.

"Of course," I said, placing my hand on his shoulder. "You would sit on the front row with Tammy and me, and you'd be our honored guest. We would love for you to join us."

He grinned like a teenager contemplating an invitation to his first school dance. "Thank you, Pastor," he said. "You are most kind. I would love to!"

When I returned to Joe's shop about ten days later for my final fitting, he beamed when he saw me and introduced me to his cousin, a man only a few years younger than himself. After pleasantries were exchanged, I gently revisited my invitation for Joe to visit our church some time. Unexpectedly, his cousin asked if he might be able to come as well.

"Yes, we would love to have you both," I said.

"Thank you, Pastor!" they said in unison, shaking my hand and looking as though I had invited them to the Super Bowl instead of to a sermon series.

Correct but Not Helpful

As I've thought about this experience, I've wondered why Joe and his cousin responded so differently to my invitation than they did in their prior encounters with Christians, especially when all our offers were essentially the same. I respect and admire the person Joe ate dinner with as a strong man of God. Upon reflection, though, I realized his style of sharing the gospel tends to be more confrontational than mine. While I agree with this pastor's beliefs, I question his technique. In his approach to Joe, he was *correct* but he wasn't *helpful*. Joe walked away from their conversation feeling the door had been slammed in his face.

And that's the problem. Often we mean well, but we don't love well. In every single encounter Jesus had with people, we see an unwavering attitude of love even as he called them to leave their sin behind and follow him. My favorite example of this takes place with the woman caught in adultery.

The Jewish religious leaders had dragged this poor woman from her lover's bed into the streets where they confronted Jesus, reminding him that the woman's punishment, according to the Law of Moses, was death by stoning. These Pharisees wanted to trap Christ between the old law, which was the traditional path to righteousness before God, and the new grace that he had been preaching. But Jesus' response literally left them speechless:

> They kept demanding an answer, so he stood up again and said, "All right, but let the one who has never sinned throw the first stone!" Then he stooped down again and wrote in the dust.
>
> When the accusers heard this, they slipped away one by one, beginning with the oldest, until only Jesus was left in the middle of the crowd with the woman. Then Jesus stood up again and said to the woman, "Where are your accusers? Didn't even one of them condemn you?"
>
> "No, Lord," she said.
>
> And Jesus said, "Neither do I. Go and sin no more." (John 8:7–11 NLT)

Don't you just love Jesus' response here? He doesn't condemn the woman like the religious legalists; instead, he shows her grace. But he doesn't let her off the hook either; he tells her to "go and sin no more." Jesus avoids the extremes of either-or by displaying both love *and* righteousness.

I hold his example close as a model of how to interact with the diverse people I encounter with increasing frequency. Whether it's someone like my friend Joe who has a different cultural background, a same-sex couple who moves into our neighborhood, or a liberal activist wanting to debate a topic on which we disagree, the challenge remains the same: how to stand firm *and* love well at the same time.

Here's what we need to remember: Truth without grace is mean. Grace without truth is meaningless. Truth and grace together are good medicine. And that's what this book is all about.

Calm in the Cultural Storm

Today, perhaps more than ever, we have the privilege of loving others and offering them God's truth that we're all sinful and in need of a Savior. This is exactly why Jesus came to live as a man—yet perfectly—and die on the cross. His sacrifice makes it possible for us to find hope in a relationship with a holy God. Once we experience his forgiveness and begin living in the freedom of God's grace, we're responsible to share this good news with everyone around us—no matter who they are or how different from us they may be.

> Truth without grace is mean. Grace without truth is meaningless. Truth and grace together are good medicine.

This responsibility means we balance the truth of the standards in God's Word with the reality of his loving acceptance and life-changing grace. In other words, we are to do what Jesus did with the woman caught in adultery. Living out a balanced approach isn't easy, and it almost always stretches us beyond our comfort zones. Often, the tension between standing firm and loving well paralyzes us. We want to demonstrate the love of God to others, to serve those in need, and to share the good news of the gospel with those apart from God, but we don't want to embrace the immorality that often seems to cause and emerge from so many rapid cultural changes.

Consequently, we feel like we don't know our place anymore. We're frustrated or even confused, torn between what we hear in church and what we see online. We feel caught between extremes, not wanting to alienate people who need God just as much as we do, and not wanting to compromise our convictions and biblical beliefs.

We have questions with no easy answers:

- What's my role as a follower of Jesus in today's constantly shifting culture?
- How can I stand firm in my faith and still be relevant to people who seem so different from me?
- How should I respond when others say my Christian views are unloving?
- How does the Christian message apply to everyone when there are so many differences in culture, ethnicity, lifestyle, orientation, political beliefs, and spiritual practices?
- Is the entire Bible still relevant, or are some parts culturally outdated?
- Is Scripture reliable?
- Doesn't God love us all? Didn't he send his Son to die so that all may be saved?
- If I stand for truth, what will people think of me?
- How do I help my kids engage in culture without losing them to it?
- How do I handle the barrage of constant change in our world?

When culture shifts—and it always has and always will—we

tend toward the extremes, in part because they seem easier and require less of us. We may feel so angry, threatened, and frustrated that we want to withdraw from culture, attacking and condemning people who don't agree with us. Or we may become so battle weary that we're tempted to issue a blanket acceptance that avoids any cultural conflicts.

But the good news of the gospel means we don't have to become paralyzed by extremes. We can be the calm in the midst of our cultural storm. There's another response we see demonstrated in the Bible, not only by Jesus, but also by someone in cultural circumstances shockingly similar to our own. This example reveals an ordinary person thrust into extraordinary events and the challenges that forced him to maintain a faith based on God's truth and characterized by God's grace.

This person is the prophet Daniel.

Being Right or Being Righteous

If we study the life of the prophet Daniel and the dilemma he faced, we can learn to engage our culture without compromising our faith. He faced drastic differences and diversity, and endured the immorality and corruption of a shifting culture that closely resembles our own. He not only persevered through the slippery morals and rebelliousness of his own people, but Daniel remained steadfast when thrust into one of the most decadent cultures in all of history—ancient Babylon.

Here's how it happened: After the reigns of King David and his son Solomon, Israel splintered along geographical and tribal lines. Within a few generations, the ten northern tribes of Israel abandoned their faith in the living God and started worshipping idols. Obviously, God wasn't pleased and sent warning after warning to the northern kingdom, only to have them ignored. Finally, their disobedience left him no choice; he allowed the Assyrians to conquer all ten tribes in the northern kingdom (see 2 Kings 17).

Judah, including the smaller tribe of Benjamin, comprised the southern kingdom, where Daniel lived. Despite watching what happened to their northern kinsmen, the remaining people of Israel also drifted away from God. Again, God issued the same kind of warnings through his prophets—Jeremiah, Habakkuk, and Zephaniah. But the nation of Judah refused to hear the messages of these men.

This time judgment arrived in the form of the Babylonians under the leadership of their emperor Nebuchadnezzar. Having already conquered Assyria and Egypt, they descended on Judah and decimated the city of Jerusalem. They not only looted the temple but also enslaved the Jewish people. Judah crumbled, and the people of Israel became prisoners of war in an alien culture, exiled from their homeland.

Daniel was one of these exiles. He was probably around sixteen years old when he was transported along with thousands of other Jews to be slaves in Babylon. His situation was as bleak as it gets. There was no leader organizing a secret revolt, no legal recourse or government appeal to help him. Logically speaking, Daniel had no hope.

And yet because he served God he never despaired and never gave up. Daniel had no one else, yet still he trusted God to see him through. With humble confidence, Daniel glorified God through his actions and speech. His character and conduct stood out because it was both respectful and resolute. He didn't conform to the demands of Nebuchadnezzar and all the pagan customs of the Babylonians, but he didn't act self-righteous, judgmental, or defensive either. He knew the goal wasn't to be right; *it was to have influence.* He knew being right and being righteous are not the same.

For the next seventy years of his life, Daniel faced life-threatening tests—from watching friends endure a fiery furnace to spending the night in a lions' den. But even when the foreign culture shifted around him, Daniel never wavered in his faith.

In response to Daniel's steadfast faith and commitment to both truth and grace, God demonstrated his supernatural power and honored the one who honored him by blessing Daniel with the respect of four different Babylonian emperors. Finally, the last one, Cyrus, granted the Jewish people freedom so they could return home.

Now that's influence!

Catalysts for Change

Daniel stood firm and loved everyone around him—just as Jesus did. Just as we're called to do when culture shifts. I know it's not easy to balance truth and grace in the midst of such drastic cultural change. It's easier to disengage and try to avoid culture altogether. It's easier to judge and condemn those who don't agree with us. And it's just as easy to acquiesce and accept anything and everything. But that's not what we're called to do or who we're called to be. While God calls us to be his people set apart, he also commands us to go into all the world and share the good news of Jesus Christ.

The same problems that existed in biblical times continue to challenge us today: How can we remain anchored in our Christian faith when the white water rapids of cultural change threaten to carry us away? How do we respond when culture shifts? Do we shift with it and "go with the flow"? If not, how do we interact meaningfully with a world that seems upside down to everything we believe?

From the day Daniel arrived in Babylon, he stood strong in

his faith. His example shines across the centuries and provides us with a clear model of how to live a godly life in an evil culture. We don't have to compromise our beliefs or actively participate in an "anything goes" mindset. Nor do we have to sacrifice respectful relationships with others by judging and condemning them.

> How can we remain anchored in our Christian faith when the white water rapids of cultural change threaten to carry us away?

We can find a balance between bowing down and being a doormat and becoming hardened into a ramrod of self-righteousness. But avoiding these extremes requires humility, compassion, and dependence on God. It won't be easy. We will only reflect who he truly is, both his holy righteousness and his gracious love, by relying on his Spirit to guide us.

Like the prophet Daniel, you and I can become catalysts for redemptive change in our time. We can be people of influence who know our goal is not to be *right* but to be *effective*. We can be people who stand out because of the way we relate to others, especially those different from us. We can be people who serve those in need with a willing spirit and gracious generosity. We can be people who reflect the loving-kindness of a good God.

We can be people who stand firm *and* love well.

Part 1 ───────────────────────────

Culture's Greatest Impact: Confused Identities

Who Am I?

One ————————————————————————

The Attempt to Rename Me

It ain't what they call you; it's what you answer to.

—W. C. Fields

My name is Christopher Wayne Hodges.

My parents really didn't have any rhyme or reason for choosing the names Christopher or Wayne; they just liked those names and the way they sounded together. As it turns out, the name Christopher means "Christ-bearer," which seems fitting. I like the fact that my name and what I do are one and the same. Every year I have the opportunity to share the gospel of Jesus with hundreds of thousands of people. I represent Christ. I am a Christ-bearer. My name defines me accurately. It validates me. I like my name.

But it's not the name I always believed.

Growing up, I wasn't very popular. I didn't have any athletic skills, I wasn't very smart, and I was pretty shy. That led to some fairly intense bullying from those who saw me as someone they could pick on without any repercussions. I tried to avoid it, even laugh it off at times, but it didn't work. I had to do something— anything—so I decided to win friends by taking on a new persona: Mischief Maker. I'd be the one to take the dare, crack the jokes, or do the ridiculous stunt just to make the crowd laugh—and hopefully accept me.

My strategy seemed to work, for a while. I made a few kids laugh, and I got noticed. But then I began getting into trouble on a regular basis. Basically, I was trying to live out a name that wasn't who I really was. It was the name I thought I needed so I could find acceptance and be liked.

But when I turned fifteen years old, I gave my life to Jesus, and the process of healing and redeeming my name began. I discovered the calling on my life and a passion to share Christ with the world around me. Soon I had no doubt in my mind that I had been named by God—that I had a God-given identity that he knew before I was even created. But I could only be the man he created me to be if I understood and accepted my true name.

What's in a Name?

I learned the hard way that names are important. What we believe about ourselves influences every decision we make and every action we take. And that's why, when my wife, Tammy, and I started having children, we decided to be very intentional about naming our children: Sarah Beth, Michael Robert, David William, Jonathan Bryan, and Joseph Christopher.

Okay, the truth is, we just liked the name we gave our daughter, Sarah. There wasn't any deep spiritual reasoning. We're from the South and had just moved to Colorado when she was born, so we wanted something that sounded Southern. Later we discovered that Sarah means "princess," and she reflects this royal quality in every way.

When we started naming the boys, we came up with a formula: a biblical or Hebrew first name followed by a family name.

- Michael (after the archangel) Robert (after my dad)

- David (after the giant-slayer, psalmist, and king) William (after Tammy's dad)
- Jonathan (after David's best friend) Bryan (after my grandfather Alvin Bryan)
- Joseph (after the son of Jacob in Genesis) Christopher (after me)

Curiously enough, we've noticed over the years that each of our boys embodies the traits of both the Bible character and the person in the family for whom they're named. Coincidence? Maybe. But there is something to this name thing.

Of course, we all have names. Whether or not we reflect the characteristics of our given names at birth is not the point. What matters most is the name we have written on our hearts and minds. It's what we believe about ourselves and then live out.

Maybe you were labeled "stupid" or "fat" as a kid, and despite earning a college degree or running 5Ks, you still see yourself based on those childhood labels.

Perhaps you've let sickness define you. Cancer or diabetes or MS is not only your disease, but it's also become your identity.

You might let your relationships define you. You're a husband or wife, an ex, a sister or brother, a boss, an employee.

Perhaps rejection, divorce, and betrayal have become your identity.

You may have let circumstances determine your name. Maybe the death of a loved one, tragedy, or bankruptcy have become your identity.

What's your name right now? What are the names you secretly feel are attached to you like gum on the bottom of your shoe? It's important to identify these. The

> The names you allow to label you often title the scripts you live by.

names you allow to label you often title the scripts you live by. What you believe in dictates what you live out.

This explains why the number one goal of your Enemy, the Devil, is to attack your identity. He wants to give you a different name—one that stands in direct contrast to the name God gave you when he created you.

Identity Theft

We live in a world where people have become adept at doing what is right in their own eyes, defining their identities according to their own constantly shifting ideas. From school-age children who want to change their genders to couples of the same gender planning their weddings, it's increasingly acceptable to pursue what feels right.

"Live your own truth" has become a bumper-sticker mantra for generations conditioned to believe they are entitled to reinvent themselves and live any way they choose. Reality TV portrays how anyone can be a star—models, bachelors, chefs, home buyers, politicians, and tattoo artists—as long as they remain "true to themselves."

I can see why this idea might be appealing, this freedom to embrace the desires our hearts harbor within them. After all, if I allowed my feelings to dictate my decisions, I probably wouldn't qualify to be a pastor. Instead, I'd be trying to make as much money as possible in order to create the most comfortable, pleasurable life possible, playing golf at every great course around the world. And while I may still struggle with those desires sometimes, I know I can't trust them to determine what's ultimately best for me. God has created me and called me for *his* purposes, not my own.

No matter how much I might wish I were a millionaire golf

pro, I know that's not the life I'm called to live. The truth is, we don't have the privilege of defining ourselves, and there are limits to how far we can reinvent ourselves. Why? The reason is simple: we've already been defined by God, our Creator. God knows who he made each of us to be, and in the end his design is always better than what we come up with on our own.

Daniel understood this core truth. His faith in God tethered him to it throughout his time in captivity. Steeped in a culture that elevated sensual pleasure, idol worship, and moral decadence, the Babylonians focused on many things other than God. And as they sought to assimilate their new subjects, they tried to pull Daniel and his fellow captives into their lifestyle by casting shadows on their identities. Notice the very first thing that happened to Daniel and his friends once they arrived in Babylon:

> Then the king ordered Ashpenaz, chief of his court officials, to bring into the king's service some of the Israelites from the royal family and the nobility—young men without any physical defect, handsome, showing aptitude for every kind of learning, well informed, quick to understand, and qualified to serve in the king's palace. . . .
>
> The chief official gave them new names: to Daniel, the name Belteshazzar; to Hananiah, Shadrach; to Mishael, Meshach; and to Azariah, Abednego. (Dan. 1:3–4, 7)

In those days, when victors integrated enslaved captives into their own culture, it was customary to change the captives' names as a sign of ownership. The Israelites belonged to their captors now; no longer would they be known by their old names from their homeland. But these Babylonian names weren't simply different names; these new names were meant to obliterate the Israelites' identities.

They were a mockery to their Jewish heritage.
They turned truth inside out.
They were idolatrous names.

By comparing the original and Babylonian names of these four Hebrew young men, we get a clear picture of our Enemy's strategy, the same one he uses on us today: he labels us with a new name so he can lie to us about a false identity. Let's take a closer look at how this happened with Daniel, Hananiah, Mishael, and Azariah.

From Daniel: "God is my judge" to
Belteshazzar: "Lady, protect the king"
The first thing the Babylonians did was change the gender of Daniel's name—an inherent part of each person's identity. They also shifted the focus from God to human. With this new name, Daniel's identity, at least on paper, changed from a man held accountable by an all-powerful God to that of a woman who must protect her sovereign. In their culture, this was a terrible insult. The meaning of Daniel's new name was the antithesis of his former Hebrew name.

From Hananiah: "Yahweh has been gracious"
to Shadrach: "I am fearful of God"
The Babylonians inverted the focus from God being good to God being bad. Instead of viewing him as gracious, kind, and loving (all implied by the name Hananiah), this new name echoed with the kind of fear you'd feel standing before a tyrant, a maniac, or a monster.

From Mishael: "Who can compare to my
God? No one!" to Meshach: "I am despised,
contemptible, and humiliated"

Once again, the Babylonians chose a name that subverted the goodness of God in our relationship to him. It shifted the focus from our confidence in God to cowardice.

From Azariah: "Yahweh has helped" to Abednego: "The servant of Nebo"

Azariah went from being a son or heir of Yahweh, a term of endearment for the living God, to being the slave of another man.

As you can see, in every case, the Hebrew captives' new names obliterated the true nature of God that had been represented by their names and reoriented their identities to become people who served their Babylonian masters.

Let's review these shifts in identity:

HEBREW NAME/ MEANING	BABYLONIAN NAME/MEANING	SHIFT
Daniel: "God is my judge"	Belteshazzar: "Lady, protect the king"	Male⇨female Focus on God⇨focus on man All-powerful God⇨God/ king who needs protecting
Hananiah: "Yahweh has been gracious"	Shadrach: "I am fearful of God"	Gracious, loving God⇨tyrannical God to be feared Focus on God⇨focus on self
Mishael: "Who can compare to my God? No one!"	Meshach: "I am despised, contemptible, and humiliated"	Focus on God⇨focus on self Confidence⇨cowardice
Azariah: "Yahweh has helped"	Abednego: "the servant of Nebo"	Son of God⇨slave of man

We don't have to ponder for long to realize our Enemy's attempt to make this kind of inside-out identity change continues all these years later. Daniel, Hananiah, Mishael, and Azariah were subjected to new names that rejected the truth about who God is and who they were in light of that. We still see the Enemy looking for opportunities to cast confusion on God's goodness and our identities today.

Consider, for example, the way society continues to redefine gender, gender relationships, and marriage, which is reminiscent of the gender change in Daniel's renaming. Things that were once inherent to who we are have now become flexible and up for debate. Our culture claims these qualities can be shaped to suit what a person wants with no regard for God's original design. But you and I know this is not true! There is purpose in how God makes us, and we must clearly know who we are in Christ to stand firm instead of acquiescing to who our culture says we should be.

Another way the Enemy tries to change our identities is by making it seem foolish to remain faithful to God. In Daniel's day, this attempt to shift perceptions about God was approached in a tribal way, often through conquest and assimilation. These days it's done through many different methods, from comedy and satire to controversy and scandal within the church. If the Devil can discredit the Bible and disgrace the church through division, dissension, and immorality, then he's succeeded.

As a result, most Christians today are intimidated by the world. We've become convinced we should keep our faith private, relegated to church one day a week. The world is so bold in expressing its multitude of beliefs, convictions, and "personal truths," while Christians are shamed into silence, so embarrassed by their faith that they become apologetic in a way that has nothing to do with sharing the gospel.

This is exactly what our Enemy wants to accomplish through a cultural identity change. He wants to distract us from focusing on our relationships with God and instead get us to focus on pleasing others, being enslaved to their approval. It's easy to get caught up in the number of likes, Facebook friends, positive comments, and retweets we can accumulate. It feels good to have this seemingly clear proof that we have value, that our choices have value, that they are right. It's intoxicating, this twenty-four-hour access to continual validation.

I struggle with the desire to please others as much as anyone. We might have an amazing service on Sunday with record-breaking attendance and more than a hundred decisions for Christ, and yet it only takes one negative, critical e-mail about that service to ruin my day. Instead of giving God glory for all the wonderful things that happened in that service, I get hung up wondering what I could do to please that one person who didn't like our church. I have to remind myself it's not about what I'm doing; it's about what God's doing through me, through others, through the church.

> Our identities shift when we value those looking at the art more than the Artist.

Otherwise, this shift in focus, this distraction, this change in who we orient our lives around, accomplishes the exact same thing as the changing of captives' names in ancient Babylon. Our identities shift when we value those looking at the art more than the Artist.

Your New (Old) Name

When culture shifts, we need to know who we are. Scripture tells us this truth: "Before I formed you in the womb I knew you, before you were born I set you apart; I appointed you as a prophet to the nations" (Jer. 1:5). You are who God made you to be. You are a unique, beloved child of the Lord of the universe, your

Creator, Redeemer, and Savior. You have a unique purpose for your life that no one else has had or will ever have. You are a co-heir with Jesus, adopted into the family of the King and granted eternal life with him in heaven after your mortal life on earth has ended (Rom. 8:17). This is your true identity.

Unless we're grounded in who God made us to be, the way we see ourselves will easily morph into an illusion—a cultural mirage. The truth of who we are will still be unshaken, but it will be covered with a veneer of lies. How does this happen? We lose sight of our God-given identity and act according to an off-kilter mental self-portrait: "For as he thinks in his heart, so *is* he" (Prov. 23:7 NKJV).

Our Enemy has become adept at convincing us to accept false labels. First, he gets us to accept cultural definitions of who we are. When we do, others around us get to create the standards for how we measure up—or more often, how we don't.

From peer pressure to cultural standards of beauty and success, our society continually directs our focus to external qualities. Stereotypes, or labels for people largely based on their appearances, rely on the same strategy. They reduce us to the lowest common denominator until we see ourselves, and eventually others, as only a redneck, a blonde, plus-sized, or disabled. These may be our physical characteristics, some of which affect our perspectives and worldviews, but they don't define who we are. Many of us would say we know that, but if we hear people tell us often enough that we're no good because of some trait, then we may start to believe it, however subconsciously.

Another way the Enemy utilizes false labels is by convincing us to allow our past to define who we are. He calls us "liar" or "hypocrite," "failure" or "unclean." This is the big one—the struggle so many of us have that drags us down and undermines our faith. We overlook the fact that God knows every moment of our past and loves us as if he didn't. In fact, he wants to redeem our past, but too often we get in the way because we refuse to let go of our old labels.

The glorious truth is that when we let God control our lives, he gives us a new identity. We see this gift displayed in the Bible in the way God so frequently changed the names of those people who encountered his love and forgiveness in a dramatic way. Jacob went from being a coward, who deceived his father and conned his brother out of his birthright, to being Israel, the nation of God's chosen people. Abram went from being a wandering nomad with a problem telling the truth, to Abraham, an unlikely father at an old age whom God blessed for all generations. Then there were Peter (Simeon) and Paul (Saul) in the New Testament—two more examples of new identities proclaimed by new names.

Actually, these identities were not really new; they were the ones Israel, Abraham, Peter, and Paul were always supposed to have. They just hadn't fully stepped into who God had made them to be until God marked them and called them by new names. And it wasn't until they gave up trying to control their own lives that they realized the fulfillment of who they'd been born to be.

This is certainly true in my own experience. I felt insecure and uncomfortable around people as I was growing up, so I compensated by acting out and trying to be funny all the time. And it wasn't until I faced my fears

> God doesn't see what you are based on where you are now; he sees what you can become based on where he wants to take you.

and trusted God with them, wanting his approval more than anyone else's, that I felt the freedom to preach, teach, and be the leader God created me to be.

In almost every name-changing story in the Bible, after an encounter with God, a person's identity becomes more authentically revealed. They experience the freedom to stop living by cultural constraints and to start living in spiritual freedom. And the same can be true for us. God doesn't see what you are based on where you are now; he sees what you can become based on where he wants to take you. He knows the actualities, but he sees possibilities. He recognizes what you're capable of doing and activates the greatness in you that you don't see in yourself. When you give him control of your life, he'll give you back your name!

All the Wrong Places

I recently had surgery on my shoulder to repair my rotator cuff, and it took me a few months to recover. During this time, I couldn't enjoy one of my favorite pastimes: playing golf. My need for surgery and the length of my recovery also forced me to confront my age and realize my body is not the same as it used to be.

As I started thinking about aging, suddenly I saw a new gray hair every morning when I looked in the mirror. I also noticed a few wrinkles that I didn't remember seeing before. My surgery made me slow down, and when I did, my eyes were opened. While I still thought of myself as a relatively young man, my body had started sending me some other signals.

Suddenly, I understood why some people experience this reality called a midlife crisis and do everything in their power to fight the onset of age. Maybe they have plastic surgery or begin coloring their hair. Some trade in their family sedan for a sleek new sports car. Others even go so far as to divorce their spouses and find much younger partners. All in an attempt to avoid something natural and inevitable.

It does make sense, though. When we're not connected to our God-given identities, we will plug in to other outlets to define ourselves. For some of us, it's our physical appearance and an attempt to remain beautiful and youthful. But the truth is: we all get older and life takes its toll on us. Scripture reminds us that real beauty emanates from the inside. "The LORD does not look at the things people look at. People look at the outward appearance, but the LORD looks at the heart" (1 Sam. 16:7).

Others of us define ourselves based on performance. We might experience a sense of self-worth only when people validate us for what we do and how we do it. We try to impress others with our latest achievement, award, or accomplishment. But it's never enough; no matter how much we achieve or how famous we become, the emptiness inside remains. "Yet when I surveyed all that my hands had done and what I had toiled to achieve, everything was meaningless, a chasing after the wind; nothing was gained under the sun" (Eccl. 2:11).

It's only after we embrace our true identities that work becomes purposeful and meaningful—perhaps because we know we're not defined by our performance. We do our best and can take satisfaction in giving our all regardless of the outcome. We don't have to win a gold medal, become a millionaire, or launch a nonprofit to know our self-worth. We're God's beloved sons and daughters—period! There's nothing we have to do to earn God's love, forgiveness, or grace. He gives them freely. "For it is by grace you have been saved, through faith—and this is not from yourselves, it is the gift of God—not by works, so that no one can boast" (Eph. 2:8–9).

Finally, many of us attempt to define ourselves by our possessions and monetary worth. We let money rule our lives and try to enjoy the fleeting moments of false security based on the number in our bank accounts or market portfolios. Unfortunately, money sometimes only insulates us from discovering who we really are. We might have everything money can buy but still feel disappointed by our lives. We learn the hard way that "life does not consist in an abundance of possessions" (Luke 12:15).

Let me just stop here and say, if you've ever placed your identity in your physical appearance, performance, possessions, or anything else, you are not alone. We have all found ourselves grasping at things other than God to fill the deep places of our hearts only meant for him. But if we recognize this, we can continue to work toward staying connected to the God who made us, knows us, and loves us. To become anchored by the knowledge of who God made us to be, we must see ourselves the way he sees us.

How do we do this? Perhaps the first step in this process is recognizing the biblical truth that every person is born for a specific season. "From one man he made all the nations, that they should inhabit the whole earth; and he marked out their appointed times in history and the boundaries of their lands" (Acts 17:26).

God chose us and has always loved us. He determined when we would be born and when we will die. "For he chose us in him before the creation of the world to be holy and blameless in his sight" (Eph. 1:4). We can take comfort in knowing that our Father specifically chose this place in all of time and history for our lives to exist.

You can also rest in the knowledge that within your unique identity, you have a very specific purpose. Not only did God create you to live in this particular season, but he gave you just the right personality, abilities, talents, and gifts to accomplish what you're called to do. You are not an accident. You are here on purpose for a purpose. And once you know your purpose in life, you will more clearly understand your true identity. Then nothing can stop you. Others may try to apply labels of their own, and some may even seem accurate, but when you live out of your God-given identity, these false labels can't stick. Your awareness of being the person God made you to be permeates everything you do, every decision you make, and every risk you take. Purpose is your identity in action. It reflects your identity and helps you understand it more clearly.

We see this in the lives of several biblical characters. From the time Moses was a baby saved from death by his wily mother and Pharaoh's daughter, he knew God had created him for a special purpose. Even when Moses balked at being a leader because of his fears and insecurities, he couldn't deny God's presence

> Purpose is your identity in action.

in his life and the unique ways God guided him. Pharaoh thought he could contain the Hebrew people under Moses' leadership, but God clearly knew otherwise. Ultimately, God called Moses to be a deliverer, even as Moses' cultural circumstances tried to derail him from living out this purpose.

Raised as an Egyptian prince, which many might consider a positive label, Moses couldn't escape his Hebrew heritage. Then, later on, living as a fugitive and a wanted criminal (obviously a bad label) Moses still couldn't hide from God, who spoke his calling to him directly through the burning bush. Even when Moses protested with excuses about his stutter and inability to speak publicly, he couldn't deny who God made him to be. He was eventually compelled to obey God and lead as the deliverer he had been fashioned to be (Ex. 2–4).

Joseph's life also demonstrated this same inescapable sense of purpose and identity, even as he lived through some terrible trials. Despite being sold into slavery by his brothers and jailed for a crime he didn't commit, Joseph didn't simply accept whatever new identities his captors pressed on him. He remained faithful and allowed God to use him and his gifts. While Joseph might have been tempted to allow his harsh circumstances to define him and his purpose, instead he kept his faith in God and remained obedient to be the man God created him to be. And, you'll recall, Joseph's faithfulness was rewarded as he saved the people of Egypt and Israel during the terrible famine God had revealed to him beforehand (Gen. 37–47).

How about you? Have you seen your purpose, your true identity, emerge yet? If you already know your God-given purpose, then I celebrate with you and encourage you to press on. Take comfort during challenging times and trust God to see you through them, knowing you are exactly where he wants you to be, doing what you were made to do. And if you're still searching for your divine purpose, then keep seeking what God has for you. Don't give up until he reveals to your heart your special mission in this life. Remember what's true: "For we are his workmanship, created in Christ Jesus for good works, which God prepared beforehand, that we should walk in them" (Eph. 2:10 ESV).

Finally, to own the fullness of your identity in Christ, consider how you can help the people around you be true to their own God-given identities. I'm not talking about telling them who *you* think they should be but rather looking for opportunities when another person's pain, discomfort, or current struggle results from not knowing who God made them to be. Jesus set us free so that we can help liberate others, but often this means beginning more subtly instead of storming in like soldiers on a black ops mission.

Maybe it's helping your kids think through the enormous peer pressure they're under, listening carefully before sharing some of your own experiences at their age along with the timeless truth of God's Word about pleasing God rather than people. It might be having coffee with a friend who seems to be experimenting with her lifestyle, again only so you can listen to her heart and the pain she carries there. Perhaps it's grabbing lunch with a guy from your small group who has hinted at his battle to remain faithful to his wife.

Just remember: we all struggle to remember our true identities. Almost everyone around us is carrying some secret, some burden, some painful weight when we encounter them. We don't want to force ourselves on them and intrude, but we can make ourselves available to listen and to care. Listening and caring are fundamental building blocks we must have if we're ever going to establish a strong, respectful relationship in which to share God's truth.

The rapids of culture will always try to sweep us downstream, away from who God created us to be. And the Enemy of our souls will always look for opportunities to undermine our true identities as God's divinely designed children. All the more reason to dwell on the certainty of who God says we are and to be motivated by living out the purpose for which he made us. This lifeline of truth will keep us afloat no matter how high cultural waters may rise.

No one can name you, or rename you, no matter what.

God knows who you are.

But you need to know too.

And now you can help remind others who they really are as well.

Two ─────────────────────────────────

THE STRATEGY TO TAME ME

Sir, my concern is not whether God is on our side; my greatest
concern is to be on God's side, for God is always right.

—ABRAHAM LINCOLN

Have you seen this?" my friend, a fellow pastor, asked. He
held out an image on his phone screen.

"No. What is it?" I said.

"Just take a look," he replied solemnly.

I was in Australia, along with many other ministry leaders,
to attend the annual Hillsong Conference. Invited to speak at the
Hillsong City Campus in downtown Sydney, I was waiting in the
greenroom backstage before the service. When I saw the photograph on my friend's phone, I felt like I'd been punched in the
gut. For a long few seconds, I was literally speechless.

It was a devastating iconic image that proudly pointed to our
own choice to reject God: a nighttime photograph of the White
House, home to the president of the United States of America,
illuminated in rainbow-colored floodlights. The display had been
assembled in celebration of the landmark US Supreme Court ruling the previous day allowing same-sex couples the legal right to
marry. The picture had been taken the night before and broadcast
around the world. To me, it looked like our country was thrusting

20

its middle finger toward heaven, declaring that we, not God, knew what was best and had the right to decide.

My heart was broken.

Buffet in Babylon

That moment, as I stared at that photograph, feeling sick inside, I knew I had to write this book. The rainbow-hued image of the White House was only the latest in a string of incidents and events that played out a theme I had been observing for many years: popular culture will always try to tame us into compromise and compliance with its fast-moving trends. Culture grinds against our values until either they crumble or we stand up and counter the cultural erosion.

If we want to live a godly life in the middle of all this friction, we must determine our core convictions according to the Bible and know how to live them—*before* we face the weight of social pressure from the people around us. It's always easier to resist the winds of change if your roots run deep in God's truth.

Daniel and his friends knew this firsthand. After their Babylonian captors changed their names, their new master, Ashpenaz, did something else significant: he assigned them a portion of the king's table. You might be tempted to think, *That doesn't sound so bad— what's the big deal? Maybe old Ash was just being hospitable.*

> It's always easier to resist the winds of change if your roots run deep in God's truth.

But think again. Not only did the king's rich food and drink violate the dietary laws of Israel, but most of it had been offered up to idols prior to being served.

Instead of tucking in and enjoying what must have been a sumptuous meal, "Daniel resolved not to defile himself with the royal food and wine, and he asked the chief official for permission not to defile himself this way" (Dan. 1:8). To remain pure in body and spirit, Daniel politely refused the king's sacrificial filet and cabernet. He asked instead if he and his friends could have veggies, grains, and water.

Daniel knew the kind of nourishment his soul needed as well as his body, and he knew how he was to live out his convictions. So when the opportunity to compromise came, he didn't think twice.

When you know what's in your core, you don't struggle to decide.

Decide Before the Dilemma

Receiving new names and being invited to eat at the king's table may, on the surface, have seemed like welcoming acts, but they were, in fact, the start of a full-scale assault on the young Jewish men and their faith, much like the broader scheme the Devil uses in our lives to convince us to compromise our standards. Using the shifting sands of culture, the Enemy tries to erode our convictions and change our behavior. If he can lure us into the forbidden, often by appealing to our sensual appetites, then he's derailed our relationship with God and undermined our divine purpose.

> When you know what's in your core, you don't struggle to decide.

Often the Devil's snares are open and obvious, but that doesn't make them less tempting. For instance, every January I join with many others from our church for three weeks of prayer and fasting, something we call the 21 Days of Prayer. Following the hectic holiday season, my New Year's fast has become a sacred time for me to draw closer to God and seek his guidance.

And you know what? Every year, precisely during that precious time of prayer and fasting, I'm asked to speak and preach in some of the most beautiful, exotic, and amazing places in the world: tropical retreats, European conferences, Australian churches, and African missions. They're almost always worthwhile events that normally I'd love to be a part of, and they're almost always set in a place I either love or have always wanted to visit. But I refuse to give up what I know God wants me to do. Before those invitations come in, I make sure to block out the month of January for my most important appointment of the entire year.

The Enemy will use all kinds of enticements to pull you away from God's plan, to lessen your impact, to try and tame you. He'll make them seem easy and enjoyable—no big deal. Some will even seem like gifts from the Lord, blessings that look harmless to accept. But they derail you from what God actually has for you.

That's why you have to know what you stand for before that moment comes when you're offered that hit, that drink, that touch, that glimpse, that purchase, that taste. Pre-decide what you will do when those temptations come your way—and they definitely will come your way, often when you're at your weakest or when your defenses are down. Settle your core convictions and use them as anchors when everything and everyone around you wants to sweep you away.

Consider King David. He wrote, "My heart is set on keeping your decrees to the very end. . . . And because I consider all your precepts right, I hate every wrong path" (Ps. 119:112, 128). He was far from perfect, but David always found his way back to God. He knew what he believed, and not even Goliath, Saul, Bathsheba, and Absalom could shake David's faith.

Ultimately, each one of us is responsible for what we hold true within our hearts. The question is whether it's God's truth or man's truth. Culture will try to convince you that there are no absolute truths. We'll be told "it's complicated" and that truth depends on context or a person's individual situation. What we hold true will be questioned: that the Bible is God's Word, that Jesus is the Son of God, that we must be born again. We will be questioned about our ministry values and challenged on our stand on social issues like marriage and family, money, and the sanctity of life.

Moral relativism is the religion of the day. If you doubt this, just consider that only 35 percent of Americans believe in moral absolutes anymore.[1] This figure was cited by George Barna, whose firm conducted the research, as a major factor underlying the data he released in a controversial public presentation about the moral views and behaviors of Christians. In that forum Barna noted that substantial numbers of Christians believe that activities such as abortion, gay sex, sexual fantasies, cohabitation, drunkenness, and viewing pornography are morally acceptable.

> Without some firm and compelling basis for suggesting that such acts are inappropriate, people are left with philosophies such as "if it feels good, do it," "everyone else is doing it" or "as long as it doesn't hurt anyone else, it's permissible." In fact, the alarmingly fast decline of moral foundations among our young people has culminated in a one-word worldview: "whatever." The result is a mentality that esteems pluralism, relativism, tolerance, and diversity without critical reflection of the implications of particular views and actions.[2]

It is absolutely possible, slowly but surely, to be led away from what God's Word says about the hot topics of today. If we want to stand for our beliefs, especially when it's not easy or politically correct to do so, then we must have a firm grasp of the foundation of our faith and why we hold to increasingly unpopular convictions. We must, as David did, maintain an eternal point of view as our basis of reference for the cultural changes fluctuating around us.

But our goal in knowing our core convictions is not to draw a line in the sand and create an "us vs. them" mind-set. Our goal is to build bridges and serve those in need so that they might be drawn to the love of God. No one was ever won to Christ because they lost an argument. Jesus told us to share the good news of the gospel throughout all the world (Matt. 28:16–20), and he made it clear that we were to be *in* the world but not *of* the world (John 15:18–20). He said, "By this everyone will know that you are my disciples, if you love one another" (John 13:35).

We have the privilege of loving others and offering them God's truth: that we're all sinful and in need of a Savior, which is exactly why Jesus came to live as a man and die on the cross. His sacrifice makes it possible for us all to find hope in a relationship with a holy God. Amid so many negative, destructive factors at work in our culture, we offer the good news of the gospel and have the tremendous privilege of bringing light and life to everyone around us.

The way we do this without being swallowed up by cultural forces is by anchoring ourselves to a worldview based on God's Word. Knowing what we believe and why we believe it is foundational to our ability to be people of positive influence. Having God's truth as our point of reference not only allows us to withstand the swirling currents of cultural change, but it also allows us to extend a lifeline of grace to others around us.

Worldview Finder

Everyone has a worldview, a way of seeing, filtering, and processing the events of their daily lives in the context of the world they live in. Basically, your worldview is the set of beliefs that you base your life on. It is the core convictions you consider when faced with decisions. It is the lens through which you view and assess the world at large.

Many factors shape your personal worldview. We all experience many of the same life events, but we see them differently. We don't see things as they are, but as *we* are—through a filter of our personal experiences, relationships, observations, and conclusions. Both good and bad, these variables are often biased, inaccurate, and subject to our emotions.

> We don't see things as they are, but as *we* are.

This is why we have conflict and engage in arguments with each other—because everybody uses a different filter. You have your viewpoint, and I have mine. If we take five different people, each will have his or her own unique viewpoint. These people can all attend the same event but have completely different experiences and conclusions about it.

If you've ever been involved in a car accident, you probably realized that everyone else involved saw it happen a different way. One driver thinks it's the other driver's fault. The other driver thinks the accident happened because there was no stop sign at the intersection. An eyewitness thinks the collision occurred because the afternoon sun momentarily blinded one of the drivers. The officer who arrives at the scene looks at the tire marks, crumpled fender, and other evidence and reaches yet an entirely different conclusion. They're all looking at the same event from their own personal worldviews.

Our worldviews inform how we see God, how we view ourselves, and how we regard other people. They interpret our past experiences, our present circumstances, and our future expectations. Our personal worldviews affect how we see money, sex, work, and time, and even how we view good and evil.

This filter for processing everything around us influences every choice we make. If you've dated frequently and been engaged a half-dozen times but never made it to the altar, then you begin to think it unlikely you'll ever get married. Your past experiences lead you to some false conclusions: that you're not "cut out" for marriage, that others are unreliable and untrustworthy, that relationships can't last for more than a few months. If you allow these false beliefs to influence your attitude, then others don't want to be around your negativity or unwillingness to trust them. You end up reinforcing these lies of the Enemy and the cycle continues.

What we believe—about ourselves, about God, about others, about the way life works—makes a direct impact on our decisions each day. Our worldviews shape the objective events we encounter into subjective experiences. But here's the problem: our worldviews are profoundly influenced by the worldviews of others.

In fact, we probably have many ingredients baked into our worldviews that we never chose consciously or deliberately. We picked them up

> Our worldviews require truth, and if we haven't based them on God's Word, the ultimate truth, then our worldviews rely on false and negative contributions of the world.

from our surroundings, our environment, our families, and the people we're around most frequently. Every time we listen to a song, we are exposed to its worldview. Every movie or TV show we watch represents a worldview. Every time we read a newspaper, magazine, novel, textbook, blog, or tweet, we see a worldview. Every conversation, every interaction, every personal encounter. They each convey a worldview.

Consequently, many threads in the tapestry of our worldviews don't belong. They're not true. Our worldviews require truth, and if we haven't based them on God's Word, the ultimate truth, then our worldviews rely on false and negative contributions of the world.

Consider this: In the same Barna study I mentioned earlier, 62 percent of Americans polled said they considered themselves "deeply spiritual." These same people were then asked how this "deep spirituality" affected their decision making. Almost a third, 31 percent, said, "I make my moral choices based on what feels right and comfortable."

> We need to get our worldviews from a correct Wordview.

Another 18 percent of this group said, "I make moral choices based on whatever is best for me."

There's another 14 percent of Americans who said, "I make moral choices based on whatever causes the least conflict with others."

Only 16 percent reported, "I make my moral choices based on what the Bible says, what God's Word says."[3] This means most Christians have non-Christian worldviews! You may be a believer and be on your way to heaven yet still not have a Christian worldview because you got it from the world and not from the Word. If we don't base our decisions on the Bible, then there will be devastating consequences. We need to get our worldviews from a correct Wordview.

The biggest challenge to maintaining this will be that life won't always make sense. We struggle constantly with thoughts such as, *Why isn't my life working out like I thought it would? It's not what I intended it to be at all! Why do I feel so stressed all the time? Why is everything in my life such a mess? Why do my problems always overwhelm me?* And here's the short answer: we're using the wrong operating system. If we accept the world's worldview, it will mess up our lives here on earth.

Not only will we struggle unnecessarily with problem after problem, but we will also miss out on rewards God has planned for us in heaven. We will get into heaven, but because we lived according to the world's standards instead of God's, we will miss out on the heavenly rewards God wants us to enjoy for eternity.

If we want to maintain a worldview centered on Christ and live according to God's standards, then we must determine our core convictions. Just as a building must have load-bearing beams to support its structure, our worldview relies on beliefs determined by God's Word. Otherwise, when the culture-quakes of change occur, our worldview will collapse.

Core Convictions

Convictions require you to decide what's right ahead of time. They're not based on what feels good or seems right in the moment. They are, instead, the unmovable foundation upon which our lives are built. We don't need to be mean or judgmental when we share them with others, but we do need to be sure of them. Our beliefs, values, and moral convictions provide a starting point for what we think and feel, the decisions we make, and the actions we take. They shape every aspect of our lives.

We can see how our convictions influence our lives most clearly in our relationships. For instance, my wife, Tammy, and I have been married for more than thirty years, and I'm the only guy who has ever kissed her. You know what that makes me? The best kisser in her world!

Seriously, we decided early in our lives how we wanted our relationships, especially with the opposite sex, to honor God. As a result, when we married we were both virgins and could give ourselves to each other fully, knowing we got to open God's gift of intimacy together without having to compare, complain, or compete with anyone else. I've talked to many people in the church who have struggled with the aftermath of giving their sexual purity away before marriage. But the good news is, it's possible to become pure again in the eyes of God. If you've had that same struggle, know that God wants to restore you and heal you. That process can begin when you come before him, ask for forgiveness, and lift up your hurt.

Another thing Tammy and I agreed to when we got married was to take our vows as seriously as God takes them. We defined "till death do us part" as a lifetime commitment—no matter what. Consequently, we agreed to throw out two words from our dictionary: *impossible* (because it's not in God's vocabulary) and *divorce* (because it's not an option).

I won't presume to tell you exactly what your core convictions should be, since a range of different convictions can all be rooted in the Word of God, but because I'm frequently asked about my own, I would like to explore a few areas of conviction that are crucial to how one engages with the surrounding culture.

1. WORSHIP, or placing worth and value on who God is, tops my list. Scripture is crystal clear about God's preeminence, the way he surpasses all others:

> The Son is the image of the invisible God, the firstborn over all creation. For in him all things were created: things in heaven and on earth, visible and invisible, whether thrones or powers or rulers or authorities; all things have been created through him and for him. He is before all things, and in him all things hold together. And he is the head of the body, the church;

he is the beginning and the firstborn from among the dead, so that in everything he might have the supremacy. (Col. 1:15–18)

When we worship God, we embrace his attributes. We see him as omnipresent (everywhere at once), omniscient (all-knowing), omnipotent (all-powerful), totally good, and totally loving. Worship is not about responsive readings or singing hymns. Worship is surrendering yourself to the power, majesty, and goodness of your Creator, letting God be God—even when you don't understand what he's doing or when you disagree. "Therefore, I urge you, brothers and sisters, in view of God's mercy, to offer your bodies as a living sacrifice, holy and pleasing to God—this is your true and proper worship" (Rom. 12:1). When we surrender ourselves to God in all things and acknowledge his headship, we don't question him, even when the culture does.

2. GOD'S WORD, or placing worth and value on the Bible and believing it is the infallible Word of God, comes next. "All Scripture is God-breathed and is useful for teaching, rebuking, correcting and training in righteousness, so that the servant of God may be thoroughly equipped for every good work" (2 Tim. 3:16–17). With any situation you face, let God's Word settle it. Don't let society explain away what God says is true.

We must stay full of the Word of God, using it as the guiding light for our daily lives and the moral basis for our value system. We must be careful to rely solely on truth, avoiding gossip, hearsay, and the opinions of others.

When asked what I think about current events or some particular issue, I often respond, "What makes you think my opinion matters? It's what God thinks that counts."

3. HOLINESS raises the standard of personal purity as we honor the lordship of Christ. God's character, Christ's example, and the Holy Spirit's guidance provide our understanding of personal holiness. It's being set apart from the world in a way that distinctly reflects who God is and what he's about. "You know the guidelines we laid out for you from the Master Jesus. God wants you to live a pure life. Keep yourselves from sexual promiscuity. Learn to appreciate and give dignity to your body, not abusing it, as is so common among those who know nothing of God" (1 Thess. 4:2–5 MSG).

Holiness requires us to maintain a standard of salt-and-light leadership to those around us. It acknowledges God's lordship over our lives and demonstrates our willingness to follow in the sacrificial footsteps of Jesus. It means we think through our words, actions, habits, and attitudes at all times. Holiness prevents us from conforming to cultural changes and moral relativism.

4. FAMILY carries worth and value as a sacred institution created by God. We are made in his image and designed for relationship. This begins with our families and extends when we marry and start a family of our own. As children, we're instructed to honor our fathers and our mothers and to obey them; as parents, we are warned not to provoke or harm our children (Eph. 6:2–4). Families take care of one another. "Anyone who does not provide for their relatives, and especially for their own household, has denied the faith and is worse than an unbeliever" (1 Tim. 5:8).

One relationship that is central to the family is marriage. God considers marriage to be a lifelong sacred covenant between a man and a woman. He hates divorce, because marriage is designed to reflect the relationship between Christ and the church. According to Ephesians 5, husbands should love their wives as Christ loves the church, leading through sacrificial service, and wives must love their husbands with respect, honoring them through sacrificial devotion (vv. 22–26). Strong families grow out of strong marriages in which husbands and wives love and respect each other, serve and honor each other.

5. LIFE has intrinsic value in all forms, reflecting this most precious gift from God. Therefore, no person has the right to terminate human life, their own or anyone else's. "The word of the LORD came to me, saying, 'Before I formed you in the womb I knew you, before you were born I set you apart; I appointed you as a prophet to the nations'" (Jer. 1:4–5).

God knew each person even before he or she was conceived, so we must value each life as a gift from God. In light of this truth, we must face the fact that abortion is murder—there's no nice way to say it—and taking one's own life—including euthanasia and doctor-assisted suicide—is not our decision to make. Life is precious, and only God has the right to control when we live and when we die—not human beings.

6. HUMILITY reflects an attitude of service, compassion, and strength. It's the quality of placing the needs of others above your own, refusing to grandstand and draw attention to yourself. Truly humble people always reflect the glory of God, reminding us that he is the source of life. The opposite, of course, is pride—our human tendency to want the praise, adoration, and attention of those around us, to take all the credit and shift all the responsibility. Yet God's view on human pride is clear: "God opposes the proud but shows favor to the humble" (James 4:6).

Humility serves as the remedy for prideful self-centeredness. It reflects simplicity and sincerity, a willingness to sacrifice one's ego. My family and I keep our lives and our ministry simple so we can do more for God. Living simply lowers costs and frees up our time so resources can go to the work of the Lord. We reach people for the glory of God, not for our own egos. Sincerity keeps us real and touchable, and it makes sure our words and thoughts match. Humility keeps our hearts tuned to God and not ourselves.

These core areas of conviction probably don't surprise you, but if you don't know what you believe about any of them, then I encourage you to explore God's Word and commit to his truth. Culture will continue to be our Enemy's smokescreen for obscuring truth and confusing God's people. But if you keep your eyes on the firm ground of God's truth, deciding what you believe before you're tested, then you will stand strong no matter how many bow down to the cultural pressure around you.

Who Says So?

We live in a swiftly changing world, and it can be a difficult task to stay firmly grounded as everything around us shifts. But even as cultural forces attempt to influence and corrupt our biblical worldview, we must remain vigilant and accept only the beliefs and standards that align with our core convictions from the Word of God. This is why I was so upset by that picture of the White House with all the rainbow-colored lights and the Supreme Court ruling it was flaunting. The Bible is very clear about marriage: one man and one woman for life. This is God's intended original design. He even made the parts of a man's body and a woman's body to fit together and to have a purpose in fitting together. This was God's plan all along.

One question I hear a lot in response to this definition is, "But what about all the polygamy in the Bible? There were guys in the Bible who had multiple wives." To which I respond, "Not everything the Bible reports the Bible approves." In other words, not everything reported in the Bible is affirmed in the Bible by God. One example is the issue of slavery. Scripture includes historical accounts of people having slaves, yet it is clearly against slavery, all the way back to the very first books of the Bible. In fact, Jesus quoted Scripture and said he came to abolish and eliminate slavery—to release the oppressed and set people free (Luke 4:18). So just because we read something in the Bible about violence or some sexual deviation, it doesn't mean the Bible approves it. It's just accurately reporting the brokenness of humanity.

If you consider that we call it the *Holy* Bible, it's actually amazing. Why? Because you won't find a book that's got more violence, more incest, rape, molestation, murder, jealousy, and greed.

So why do we call it the Holy Bible then? Because this book tells the truth. If this were a human book, it might not report all the warts and flaws of its heroes. It would just give biographies about the good things they did—their great exploits. But the Bible, when it talks about Abraham and Moses and David, tells us all their weaknesses and demonstrates that they blew it just as much as we do. They made just as many mistakes, and their families were just as messed up as ours are. They had as many problems and addictions as everybody else. The Bible tells the truth.

Here's what God says about marriage in his Word:

> "Haven't you read," he replied, "that at the beginning the Creator 'made them male and female,' and said, 'For this reason a man

will leave his father and mother and be united to his wife, and the two will become one flesh'? So they are no longer two, but one flesh. Therefore what God has joined together, let no one separate." (Matt. 19:4–6)

From the very beginning of creation, marriage has always been one man and one woman joined for life. Who says so? Not me. God says so. While culture attempts to erode our convictions on many issues, this one remains under the rainbow-colored spotlight. It reminds us to return to our roots, our core beliefs, based on God's truth and not our own preferences. Because if we don't, we're in trouble. If we as Christians accept culture's attempts to reshape our beliefs, then our faith is built on nothing more than subjective impressions and seasonal trends. The result is not faith based on God's timeless Word but on a temporary, human-created belief system.

If we want to stand strong in a culture that consistently tells us to bow down, then we must know what we're standing on. As followers of Jesus, we're standing on eternal truth, the authority of the one and only holy God, and the power of the gospel to change lives. "This hope is a strong and trustworthy anchor for our souls. It leads us through the curtain into God's inner sanctuary" (Heb. 6:19 NLT).

Three

THE TEST TO CLAIM ME

*Every test, every trial, every heartache that's been
significant, I can turn it over and see how God
has turned it into good no matter what.*

—CHARLES STANLEY

When my daughter, Sarah, was thirteen, she came home
from school one day with something going on in her eye.
It was red and irritated, and her distress was clear. Tammy took
her to our pediatrician, who examined Sarah, quickly became
concerned, and referred her to an ophthalmologist. By this time
we were obviously worried but assumed the problem was some
kind of rare infection that could be treated with maybe a strong
antibiotic.

But the specialist explained that not only was Sarah's optic
nerve inflamed in her sore eye but the nerve was under attack,
which would cause blindness. He said that usually he only saw
this condition in patients with early onset multiple sclerosis and
referred us to a neurologist for diagnosis and treatment.

It went unsaid that MS is a chronic disease that can be managed but has no known cure.

That it could mean a shorter life expectancy at worst and dramatically lowered quality of life at best.

Seeing Clearly

As you can imagine, we were in shock. It was like going in to your doctor for poison ivy and coming out having been told it was skin cancer. I felt discouraged and afraid but tried to remain positive and strong for Sarah's sake, and Tammy's. Yet something beyond the obvious still bothered me about it all. We were hearing a lot of words like *maybe* and *possibly* but nothing definitive, absolute, certain. While I know medicine can be as much art as science, especially when diagnosing an illness, I wondered if this situation might be a spiritual attack on our family and the church. I wondered if my faith was being tested.

Now, I'm not one to look for a demon behind every bush, but something about the entire process felt strange to me. Our church was growing like never before, and we had just moved into a new facility. We were preparing to dedicate our church and launch a community event in hopes of attracting as many neighbors and newcomers as possible. Having something so drastic happen in my family so close to our launch event seemed suspicious.

Nevertheless, I felt so defeated and depressed that I canceled all my appointments and stayed home for two days. As the weekend approached, I was forced to consider what was on the docket and whether I was still going to show up despite my internal state of chaos. I had committed to attend a prayer service at church on Saturday but didn't feel like going. I had plenty of excuses to skip it, reasons my church family would have understood, but I knew I should be there—especially to share our situation and ask others to pray. So that morning I got in my car and headed toward church.

As I pulled up to a traffic light at a busy intersection, I could tell I would be sitting there awhile, and my eyes fell on my Bible on the passenger seat next to me. I casually flipped it open, wishing desperately for some kind of message from God, even though I was doing something I usually warned others not to do. God's Word is certainly not a Magic 8-ball, but I can't deny that the passage to which I flipped, 1 Corinthians 15, hit me like a lightning bolt:

> "Where, O death, is your victory?
> Where, O death, is your sting?"

> The sting of death is sin, and the power of sin is the law. But thanks be to God! He gives us the victory through our Lord Jesus Christ.
>
> Therefore, my dear brothers and sisters, stand firm. Let nothing move you. Always give yourselves fully to the work of the Lord, because you know that your labor in the Lord is not in vain. (vv. 55–58)

While I knew the first verses my eyes fell on were true—we shouldn't fret about our perishable bodies because there is a resurrection—I still didn't want Sarah to die. I didn't want to watch her suffer with such a debilitating disease that would likely claim her life prematurely. Then I lingered over verse 58, which encourages us to stand firm in our faith so that nothing can shake us, to give ourselves fully to the work of the Lord. My uneasy feeling persisted, but I made a choice right then. I decided to reaffirm my commitment to Jesus, to serve him no matter what—even in the unbearable event of losing my precious daughter.

Feeling bolstered by my encounter with God at the stoplight and by Saturday's prayer meeting, on Sunday I talked to one of our members whose father was a well-known neurologist. When I called and explained our situation to him, he graciously agreed to see us the next day. On Monday we drove down to Montgomery, and he examined Sarah and performed an MRI. He saw no signs of MS—everything looked fine! While we breathed a sigh of relief, it was only a partial victory because Sarah still couldn't see out of her left eye. The neurologist encouraged us to wait a few days and see if the eye healed on its own, and we agreed.

Later that week we hosted our first big public event at the church and had an amazing turnout. More than twenty-two hundred people attended, and more than six hundred made decisions to accept Jesus! We were so grateful to the Lord for his goodness, and we gave him thanks for how it all came together. And you know what? The next morning Sarah's vision improved! While her eye remained sore for a few more days, she had no more problems with her vision after that. Today she's totally healthy and happy and the mother of a new baby, our first grandchild.

Tried and Tested

The timing of Sarah's ailment and subsequent recovery could have been coincidental, but in this case hindsight is twenty-twenty. The entire incident clearly tested our faith right before a strategic, crucial event for God's kingdom. The Enemy used my fears and frustration over my daughter's medical situation to try to distract me from a soul-winning kingdom event. Yet God allowed it to mature my faith and to increase my trust and joy in him.

You see, the problems we face in this life are not circumstantial or random—they are opportunities to grow stronger in our faith. God allows these tests to prove our mettle and mature us for future purposes. Understanding the nature of these tests (whether they last only a few weeks or an entire lifetime) and how to respond to them can make all the difference in the world.

Knowing our identity is critical.

Settling our core convictions is too.

But, unfailingly, at some point, we will all be tested.

As we explored in chapter 2, determining our core convictions is essential to a strong, stand-up faith. But convictions alone won't insulate us from the trials that put them to the test. If a chain is only as strong as its weakest link, then the strength of our faith relies on the stability of what we believe when under attack. It requires courage to look the

> Convictions are all about the choices we make before we're challenged. Faith is our ability to act on our convictions when tested.

Enemy in the eye and stand our ground, so we need to know with confidence what our faith is built on. Convictions are all about the choices we make before we're challenged. Faith is our ability to act on our convictions when tested.

Daniel knew what it meant for his faith to be tested—repeatedly. In fact, he even asked his Babylonian captors to put him to the test. Here's how it happened:

> Daniel then said to the guard whom the chief official had appointed over Daniel, Hananiah, Mishael and Azariah, "Please test your servants for ten days: Give us nothing but vegetables to eat and water to drink. Then compare our appearance with that of the young men who eat the royal food, and treat your servants in accordance with what you see." So he agreed to this and tested them for ten days. (Dan. 1:11–14)

Daniel asked Ashpenaz to test him and his Hebrew friends for ten days. Why ten? Throughout Scripture, the number ten represents the testing of faithfulness: obeying the Ten Commandments (Ex. 20), giving a tenth to the Lord (Deut. 14:22; Mal. 3:10), praying for ten days in the Upper Room after Jesus ascended (Acts 13), enduring ten days of persecution in Smyrna (Rev. 2:10). Daniel knew that his faith would be put to the test, and he embraced the challenge. Rather than trying to avoid the discomfort of being tested, Daniel saw this conflict with culture as an opportunity.

When culture shifts, our faith will always be tested. The Enemy uses tests to wear us down in his attempt to derail our faith. He wants to place obstacles in our way and challenge our convictions. Paul encountered this and wrote, "For we wanted to come to you—certainly I, Paul, did, again and again—but Satan blocked our way" (1 Thess. 2:18). The Greek word used here for *blocked* literally means "cut a ditch" or "made a detour." When we're walking in the purposes God has for us, we go directly against the will and the plans of the Enemy. So, naturally, the Enemy wants to block our paths and convince us to give up, to take a permanent detour. Ultimately, he wants us to serve him. Whenever our faith is tested, we must choose whom we will serve.

> Whenever our faith is tested, we must choose whom we will serve.

Turn the Other Cheek

One of the clearest challenges to my faith happened when I was a student at Louisiana State University. Let me say first that the college experience, by its very nature, is one big test if you're trying to follow Jesus. Suddenly, as a young adult, you have all this juicy freedom you've never had before. You can stay out all night and sleep all day, skip classes you don't like, eat what you want when you want, go to endless parties, drink, smoke—even dance. So just being on a huge university campus like LSU challenged my faith as a young man.

But one incident still stands out to me. I had gotten a job at the LSU Law School, working in the maintenance department to make money for my living expenses. Most of the crew members were good old boys, proud rednecks who liked to smoke, drink, cuss, and make jokes about quiet Christian boys like me. I was so fervent about my faith that I decided to bring my Bible to work and read it at lunch and during breaks. The other guys just laughed and talked trash about me.

One day one of their buddies from the campus police force dropped by. He happened to be from the Middle East, a big, burly guy named Mohammad. Mohammad stopped in and saw me reading my Bible over in a corner. He joined in the jokes with the other guys at first, but then he came over and said, "You don't really believe the stuff in that book, do you?"

I looked up at him and said, "Yes, I do. I believe it's God's Word. I really do."

"No, you don't," Mohammad scoffed. "Not when push comes to shove, you don't."

"I'm afraid you're wrong," I said. "I really do believe every word in this Bible. I'm a follower of Jesus, and this helps me live my life."

"Really?" he taunted. "You'd still believe it was true no matter what happened to you?"

"Yes, absolutely," I said.

Smack! In that instant Mohammad backhanded me so hard I flew off my stool and landed on the floor. My jaw felt like it had run into a brick wall.

"Hey! What was that for?" I said, getting up.

Mohammad picked up my Bible and pointed his finger at me.

"If you believe everything this book says, then you must turn the other cheek."

I just looked at him, and time seemed to stand still.

Part of me wanted to get out of there. I mean, getting smacked around wasn't exactly in my job description. I didn't get paid nearly enough for this kind of abuse.

Part of me wanted to laugh and tell Mohammad to back off. He clearly enjoyed being a bully, and there was probably no way I could win here.

But the rest of me knew this was a test, an opportunity to stand up for Jesus in the face of adversity. So I looked Mohammad in the eye and slowly turned my face to present my other cheek to him. "Go ahead," I said.

"No, you don't mean it."

"Yes. Go ahead. Here's my other cheek."

Crack! Another set of knuckles to my face as I saw stars and stumbled backward. I stood up and picked up my Bible, which he had dropped. I sat down on my stool and started reading it, trying to ignore the blistering ache of my poor head.

Mohammad stared at me and then took off his cap. His entire demeanor had changed. Somehow I had won his respect.

"You're the first real Christian I have ever met," he said. "Tell me what you believe and why you believe it."

That encounter became the beginning of a friendship that lasted through the rest of my time at LSU. Mohammed would come by during his breaks or after shifts and ask me to tell him about my faith, about Jesus, about what it meant to be a Christian willing to turn the other cheek.

I tell you this story not because I'm such a strong believer who faced such terrible persecution. This little incident is nothing compared to the persecution so many Christians around the world face from their families, their communities, their leaders, and their governments. I still think about Mohammad and pray for him. And I still remember what my head felt like for the rest of that week. But there has never been a moment in my life that forced me to choose whether or not to follow my faith the way that one did. Jesus said we cannot serve two masters. "Anyone who chooses to be a friend of the world becomes an enemy of God" (James 4:4).

When culture shifts, you will be tested.

But never give in to the pressure.

Because it will make you stronger.

Ten Times Better

God will always use the tests in our lives to make our faith stronger and to reveal his glory to those around us. Just look at what happened next with Daniel and his friends:

> At the end of the ten days they looked healthier and better nourished than any of the young men who ate the royal food. So the guard took away their choice food and the wine they were to drink and gave them vegetables instead.
>
> To these four young men God gave knowledge and understanding of all kinds of literature and learning. And Daniel could understand visions and dreams of all kinds.
>
> At the end of the time set by the king to bring them into his service, the chief official presented them to Nebuchadnezzar. The king talked with them, and he found none equal to Daniel, Hananiah, Mishael and Azariah; so they entered the king's service. (Dan. 1:15–19)

They passed the test with flying colors. God rewarded them with knowledge and understanding. The king found them incomparable and asked them to join his inner circle. Being tested those ten days resulted in their situation being ten times better. We're always better after the testing.

And life is full of tests. Everything great is learned and earned through pain. The very act of childbirth, of coming into this world, brings great pain for both mother and child. My wife tells me there's no other pain to compare to the anguish of pushing a bowling ball–sized little person through your body. It's probably no picnic for the baby either, being pushed and pulled from the warmth and safety of the womb into a cold, loud room where someone slaps you until you scream your head off. Fortunately, we don't remember that part.

> Everything great is learned and earned through pain.

But we do remember the hard work, painful sacrifices, and countless hours poured into the birth of a career, a new business, or a ministry. When we follow God's guidance and we're living according to his purpose for our lives, we will be tested. We will be tempted to give up. To take the easy way out. To run away from the trouble. But those tests become stepping-stones to growing stronger and stronger, to becoming all that God wants us to be.

> How gracious he will be when you cry for help! As soon as he hears, he will answer you. Although the Lord gives you the bread of adversity and the water of affliction, your teachers will be hidden no more; with your own eyes you will see them. Whether you turn to the right or to the left, your ears will hear a voice behind you, saying, "This is the way; walk in it." (Isa. 30:19–21)

The way we handle adversity and affliction is key to a successful Christian life. We are all going to walk through difficult times—they're inevitable. It's how we respond that determines our faith and our rate of growth. We must learn to understand and accept tests as part of the process of maturation. It's how we grow. We're told,

> In all this you greatly rejoice, though now for a little while you may have had to suffer grief in all kinds of trials. These have come so that the proven genuineness of your faith—of greater worth than gold, which perishes even though refined by fire—may result in praise, glory and honor when Jesus Christ is revealed. (1 Peter 1:6–7)

Nearly every moment of life is a test. If we're serious about growing in our faith, we will likely experience greater testing than other people who are not following God. The Bible calls it the "refiner's fire" (Mal. 3:2). This refers to the process that blacksmiths and other metal workers use to improve the quality of their work. They heat up the metal to reveal its impurities, which they then remove to make the metal purer and fitter for its purpose.

> God tests us to refine us—not to punish us.

God tests us to refine us—not to punish us.

Pop Quiz

You remember how your schoolteachers would surprise you with a pop quiz, an unscheduled and usually unexpected test? Those tests weren't necessarily fun, but they were good indicators of what and how we were learning. Daily life is full of those same kinds of pop quizzes. Every day we face opportunities to exercise and grow in our faith. Spiritual testing is basically God's pop quiz, a challenging situation or unexpected circumstance that reveals our potential, growth, and maturity.

Many of us interpret resistance the wrong way. We can often view tests as nothing more than an attack of the Devil—but that's not the case. The Enemy may try to attack us while we're in the middle of a test, hoping we'll be weaker and more vulnerable; but the kind of tests we're talking about here are chances to grow, be promoted, and graduate to the next level. They're not obstacles to be despised but instead are opportunities for advancement. In fact, they may mean you're closer than ever to doing exactly what God has called you to do. Paul wrote, "I only know that in every city the Holy Spirit warns me that prison and hardships are facing me" (Acts 20:23).

After facing numerous tests and trials in his life and ministry—everything from shipwrecks to jail cells, not to mention murderous crowds—Paul knew the value of these situations. He said, "Not only so, but we also glory in our sufferings, because we know that suffering produces perseverance; perseverance, character; and character, hope" (Rom. 5:3–4). Later, he also encouraged us to "be joyful in hope, patient in affliction, faithful in prayer" (Rom. 12:12).

And Paul wasn't the only one with this counterintuitive message. James, the half-brother of Jesus, explained, "Consider it pure joy, my brothers and sisters, whenever you face trials of many kinds, because you know that the testing of your faith produces perseverance. Let perseverance finish its work so that you may be mature and complete, not lacking anything" (James 1:2–4). We can only grow in our faith if we're tested—it's that simple. It might not be what we want to hear, but it's true.

Long before Paul and James, David also saw the value of tests and welcomed them: "Test me, LORD, and try me, examine my heart and my mind" (Ps. 26:2). Like Daniel, David asked to be tested: "Search me, God, and know my heart; test me and know my anxious thoughts. See if there is any offensive way in me, and lead me in the way everlasting" (Ps. 139:23–24). How often do you pray and ask God to test you? More frequently it's the other way around for many of us—we want God to spare us from trouble and remove all obstacles from our paths. But when we ask for that, we're essentially praying that we won't grow.

Solomon, the wisest man who ever lived, reminded us, "The crucible for silver and the furnace for gold, but the LORD tests the heart" (Prov. 17:3). If we want to grow, we can't back away from places where we see our faith clashing with the culture around us. Instead, we can view that friction as an opportunity for our faith to be tested.

Embrace that conflict with the courage of the Lord.

The Heart of the Matter

It's no surprise that courage often fuels our ability to endure tests and overcome obstacles. Courage is the condition of your heart that allows you to believe you'll succeed without knowing *how* you'll succeed. But where does courage come from? The origins of the word itself reveal the way courage is forged in the depths of our souls. The English word *courage* evolved from *cour*, the Middle English word meaning "the heart," the seat of one's deepest feelings. This usage evolved from Old French, *corage*, and originally from the Latin word for "heart," *cor*.

Notice the way *core* and *courage* both come from this word for the heart. This makes sense because our hearts are the battleground between our trials and our convictions. They square off in a showdown to determine what remains and stays true in our hearts. When culture challenges our convictions, we must exercise courage—a deep-seated strength of heart—and resist the temptation to conform or compromise. Courage fuels our ability to carry out our convictions.

Where does our courage to stand strong in the face of cultural change come from? The same place where Daniel's, Abraham's, and Paul's came from: the presence of God and the Word of God. It's the same place David found courage when faced with losing all that he loved—his wives, his children, his crown, and the respect of all who followed him.

> David and his men reached Ziklag on the third day. Now the Amalekites had raided the Negev and Ziklag. They had attacked Ziklag and burned it, and had taken captive the women and everyone else in it, both young and old. They killed none of them, but carried them off as they went on their way.
>
> When David and his men came to Ziklag, they found it destroyed by fire and their wives and sons and daughters taken captive. So David and his men wept aloud until they had no strength left to weep. David's two wives had been captured—Ahinoam of Jezreel and Abigail, the widow of Nabal of Carmel. David was greatly distressed because the men were talking of stoning him; each one was bitter in spirit because of his sons and daughters. But David found strength in the LORD his God. (1 Sam. 30:1–6)

David, the king and military leader of the nation of Israel, wept aloud with his men until they had no strength to weep. Apparently, many of his men allowed bitterness to set in and began to talk of stoning David for allowing such terrible events to transpire. But notice David's response: he found strength in the Lord his God. I love how the King James Version renders verse 6, saying David "encouraged himself" in the Lord.

Sounds great, right? How cool that David, at his lowest point, was able to encourage himself in the Lord. But how do we do that? It's no coincidence that David's poetic lyrics in the Psalms often serve to ignite courage in our hearts. "Hear my cry, O God; attend to my prayer," he begged. "From the end of the earth I will cry to You, when my heart is overwhelmed; lead me to the rock that is higher than I" (Ps. 61:1–2 NKJV).

I'm convinced the secret to finding encouragement relies on our response—not our reaction. When something hard happens, it's tempting to react—to express our anger, fear, confusion, and frustration with no filter. We may lash out at others, blame ourselves, experience extreme anxiety, or sink into depression. But we have to do more than simply express our feelings; we must direct them to God and surrender ourselves to time alone in worship. In that time, we each must ask ourselves, "Am I responding or reacting?"

God can handle our scariest, most volatile emotions—just read through Psalms if you have any doubt—and he wants us to trust him with what's at stake. David, like Daniel, Paul, and others, was courageous because he understood the power of worship. I've learned this lesson personally as well. At times in my life, just after I received difficult news, I've retreated to my office and prayed, crying out to God and worshipping him. This practice has been my lifeline, providing the daily dose of courage I needed.

So many of our trials are skewed by our perspective. For us, our problems seem overwhelming and all-encompassing while God seems small and distant. But for God, the all-powerful and all-present Lord of all creation, our problems must seem quite small. However, when we meet him in quiet time alone together, then our perspective reaches a point of balance. We still may not be able to see beyond our problems or imagine how we'll get through them, but we know we're going to keep our eyes on Jesus each step forward.

The more time you spend with Jesus, the less time you're going to spend being intimidated by the opinions of others or worrying about your problems. Worshipping God has become the first thing I do whenever I'm faced with a loss, crisis, or major setback. This didn't always come naturally to me, but now I recognize how it has saved me so many times as I seek to stand strong in my faith. Worship is your lifeblood. It will produce courage to fuel your faith when you're being tested.

> The more time you spend with Jesus, the less time you're going to spend being intimidated by the opinions of others or worrying about your problems.

And you will be tested, my friend. The critical question is simply how you will respond: fearfully, allowing the Enemy a chance to derail your faith, or with courage to step forward and trust God with the outcome.

Culture wants to claim you—but you don't have to let it.

You have all you need to pass any test you face.

You have the courage of the Lord.

Part 2 ————————————————————————

CULTURE'S GREATEST TEST: WHOM WILL I WORSHIP?

Will I Worship God or Cultural Idols?

Four ——————————————————————————

WHEN THEY SAY I MUST

A person will worship something, have no doubt about that.
We may think our tribute is paid in secret in the dark recesses
of our hearts, but it will out. That which dominates our
imaginations and our thoughts will determine our lives, and
our character. Therefore, it behooves us to be careful what
we worship, for what we are worshiping we are becoming.

—RALPH WALDO EMERSON

The scene around me took my breath away. Thousands and
thousands of people surrounded me, and I witnessed every
act of worship mentioned in the Psalms: shouting, singing,
uplifted hands, laughter, clapping, chanting, dancing, and joyful
expressions of every variety. The volume of so many vibrant voices
escalated into a crescendo of exaltation. Men, women, teens, and
children from various socioeconomic, cultural, and educational
backgrounds united together to celebrate the immediate object of
their devotion:

The University of Alabama football team.

And this wasn't even a game against another college team!
That day I was one of more than ninety thousand people watching the spring practice game of the Crimson Tide, a scrimmage

between the crimson team and the white team. If you've ever been to a large-scale sporting event, I bet you can imagine what I was seeing. The scene before me was simply amazing. With all the preaching I do, everyday experiences quickly turn into sermon illustrations and learning opportunities. And that moment at the game was no different.

Worship Team

Something you should know about me is that I love sports, especially college football, and I root for my beloved Louisiana State University (LSU) Tigers year-round—Geaux Tigers! And keep in mind, my favorite team isn't very popular here in Birmingham, where I'm caught right in the crossfire between Auburn and Alabama, both former national champs and always contenders. I learned early in life that Southeastern Conference (SEC) football is its own denomination within the broader religion that is college sports. It's fun, and I absolutely love it as much as any of those other rabid fans around me did that day at the spring scrimmage in Tuscaloosa.

But that day I started thinking about how it's normal for us to hoop and holler, scream and shout, paint our faces and high-five total strangers at a football game (or even in our living rooms *watching* a football game), but we feel uncomfortable if someone raises their hands or sings out "Amen!" in a worship service. (I have a dream that one day the praise on Sunday at my church, Church of the Highlands, will be greater than the praise that happens in the football stadiums on Saturday.) God doesn't mind that we enjoy watching and playing sports. He minds if we don't put him first. We should really consider why we're willing to give praise to a team of athletes who don't even know us but stay silent before the God who created us. It all comes down to worship.

When I focus on worship, I'm not talking about singing praise songs in a church service, participating in a responsive reading, or praying with your small group. Those are all expressions of worship, but worship itself refers to what's going on inside your heart. Worship centers on the answer to a series of questions we all face: What matters most to me? Whom do I care about most? Who or what gets my devoted allegiance and loyalty? What's my top priority? Where does all my time, energy, and money go?

When we answer these questions honestly, we get a pretty accurate picture of where we stand with God. He created us in his own image as spiritual beings. We are made to worship, and if we're not worshipping our Creator, then we're trying to put something else in his rightful place. This is what we call *idolatry*: bowing down and offering our hearts to false gods.

Idolatry, worshipping anything or anyone instead of God, comes in many forms—not just in pagan statues and exotic shrines to false gods in the form of objects or animals. Our culture bombards us every day with alluring idols of power, money, sex, and fame, each one asking us to bow before it. If we're not anchored in Christ, if we haven't drawn our line in the sand that we refuse to cross, then our hearts can easily

> We are made to worship, and if we're not worshipping our Creator, then we're trying to put something else in his rightful place.

become seduced by cultural gods and then cave to temptation. Our Enemy can take us out of the race and rob us of the purpose, peace, and joy that God created us to experience.

But it doesn't have to be this way. When others compel us to bow before their idols, we can refuse to cross that line. Again, this isn't "us vs. them." But we do need to recognize that our hearts are pursuing different things. That way we can stand strong—no matter how much heat we face.

Just like Daniel.

Golden Oldies

As if they hadn't been through enough already, after the triumph of their test and being given a place in the king's inner circle, Daniel and his friends faced Babylonian pressure to bow down at point-blank range. There was no way for them to avoid this cultural confrontation. It was a spiritual tug-of-war: they could hold their ground or they could give up.

> King Nebuchadnezzar made an image of gold, sixty cubits high and six cubits wide, and set it up on the plain of Dura in the province of Babylon. He then summoned the satraps, prefects, governors, advisers, treasurers, judges, magistrates and all the other provincial officials to come to the dedication of the image he had set up. So the satraps, prefects, governors, advisers, treasurers, judges, magistrates and all the other provincial officials assembled for the dedication of the image that King Nebuchadnezzar had set up, and they stood before it.
>
> Then the herald loudly proclaimed, "Nations and peoples of every language, this is what you are commanded to do: As soon as you hear the sound of the horn, flute, zither, lyre, harp, pipes and all kinds of music, you must fall down and worship the image of gold that King Nebuchadnezzar has set up. Whoever does not fall down and worship will immediately be thrown into a blazing furnace." (Dan. 3:1–6)

This story packs a big wallop with a lot of spiritual lessons. We'll look at several, but let's start with one that tends to get overlooked: the king's idolatry relied on both image and sound. Old King Nebuchadnezzar not only erected a giant statue, but he ordered a band to play the royal soundtrack for his Golden Oldie. He wanted his subjects to experience the full audiovisual treatment as they bowed before his ego-inspired idol.

We shouldn't be surprised. Satan has always used sounds and images in his deceptions and temptations. Why? Because he knows that appealing to both these key senses has a greater effect than just focusing on either one alone. Wanting to be worshipped himself, our Enemy never forgets that people are designed for worship. He knows that human beings are drawn to sounds, especially to the cadence, rhythm, and harmony of music.

Music has incredible power to influence our moods and penetrate our thinking. Why do almost all movies have a soundtrack? To intensify the feeling we're supposed to experience while watching the film. Scary movies wouldn't be half as frightening without all those orchestra strings playing so ominously whenever someone looks in the closet or walks through the woods. And

> Wanting to be worshipped himself, our Enemy never forgets that people are designed for worship.

think about the lyrics to songs—how often do they get stuck in our heads? You can turn on the radio and have "Build Me Up, Buttercup" running through your mind for weeks!

When I got saved in 1978, I was fifteen. In the time between the free-love seventies and the anything-goes eighties, popular music held great power, just as it does now. In fact, one of the big messages preached in most youth groups at that time focused on the dangers of rock-and-roll. Most pop music, especially disco, contained innuendos of a sexual nature, if they weren't outright explicit. Heavy metal was becoming more mainstream with an emphasis on sex, violence, suicide, and death. Backward masking, or hidden, destructive subliminal messages, was revealed to be part of many such albums.

I knew personally the power of music and the kind of impact it had on people. My father was an accomplished organist and was frequently invited to play at churches around the country. One of my earliest memories was seeing Dad using both hands—and both feet—as he commanded a massive pipe organ and played a beautiful hymn. I must have inherited his love of music because I began taking piano lessons when I was five. I loved playing and learned quickly—so much that by age fifteen I was teaching a dozen students of my own. Classical pieces, old hymns, contemporary worship songs—I knew how they often set my heart free to worship God and feel his presence.

Steeped in such a rich background and love for music, I was naturally curious about how to regard popular music, especially rock. I wanted to honor God and not listen to anything that would cause me to struggle or give the Devil a foothold into my mind and heart. So, together with some other kids, I went to hear speakers from a traveling ministry, the Peters Brothers, present the truth about rock music. At the end of the service, many teens and young adults accepted Jesus, while others brought their old albums to burn. They wanted to renounce their former lifestyles and the dark messages they had listened to for so long. They had broken free and wanted to encourage others to do the same. Their message was extreme, and even though they received a lot of publicity that mocked their efforts, they weren't afraid to take a stand.

I was deeply moved by their message. They made a big impact on me and my listening habits. I quit listening to secular music shortly after.

Maybe this is too extreme for you, and you're thinking, *Come on, Chris—it's just some innocent fun. Yes, there's bad stuff in the mix, but all rock music isn't bad.* You may be right, but taking this stand has really helped me practice what I believe, and it has helped me create a barrier between my ears and popular culture. Why don't you try only listening to worship music this week and see what it does for your heart?

Like the Babylonians, I know there's something unique about the power of music. And I believe Satan uses it to get his message across in a way that seems harmless, like background noise. He's good at deception. Don't forget that he masquerades as an angel of light (2 Cor. 11:14), a throwback to his days as Lucifer before he rebelled against God and was expelled from heaven. Back then he was in charge of worship, and I have to think this included music. I believe worship in heaven still does.

He's with the Band

Let's look at our Enemy's background to gain a clearer understanding about worship from the way he sees it. To understand anything in Scripture, we must go back to its origin. In this case, let's turn to the three angels named in the Bible as ruling angels or "archangels." Each one represents a component of worship.

The first, Michael, shows up in response to Daniel's prayer (Dan. 10:13, 12:1) (more about this in a moment). Gabriel is another ruling angel and always brings a message, a Word from God. He appeared to Mary and announced the news about her selection as the mother of Jesus (Luke 1:26–56). Finally, there's Lucifer, the angel in charge of worship (Ezek. 28; Isa. 14). Every full encounter with God includes these same three components: prayer, the Word, and worship.

I believe these three archangels each ruled over a third of heaven as delegated by God. We know that when Lucifer fell, a third of the heavenly host of angels went with him (Rev. 12). His fall offers us insight into the attitude of humble surrender that must be present in a true worshipper's heart. Consider this passage from the prophet Isaiah:

> How you have fallen from heaven,
>> morning star, son of the dawn!
> You have been cast down to the earth,
>> you who once laid low the nations!
> You said in your heart,
>> "I will ascend to the heavens;
> I will raise my throne
>> above the stars of God;
> I will sit enthroned on the mount of assembly,
>> on the utmost heights of Mount Zaphon.
> I will ascend above the tops of the clouds;
> I will make myself like the Most High." (Isa. 14:12–14)

This passage was addressed to a man, the king of Babylon, but the message was intended for the spirit behind the man. This is similar to Jesus telling Peter, "Get behind me, Satan!" after Peter questioned why Jesus had to suffer and die (Matt. 16:23). Christ was speaking to Peter but sending a clear message to rebuke the Enemy.

In this passage from Isaiah, we see the way Lucifer (Satan) wanted to redirect worship away from God and toward himself. Isaiah points to five "I will" statements, all of them using words like *ascend* and *raise*, *exalted* and *highest*. Lucifer wanted to take God's place as the deity, the Most High, worthy of worship from all creation. This seems to be his greatest desire—to be exalted and lifted up in worship. He even wanted Jesus to bow down and worship him (Matt. 4:9)!

It's also interesting to note that Lucifer was described as

WHEN THEY SAY I MUST

having "stringed instruments": "Your pomp is brought down to Sheol, and the sound of your stringed instruments" (Isa. 14:11 NKJV). Another rendering of this same verse indicates that these may have been harps: "All your pomp has been brought down to the grave, along with the noise of your harps" (NIV).

In another passage, this one from the prophet Ezekiel, we find a message addressed to the king of Tyre but once again talking about Lucifer.

> You *were* the seal of perfection,
> Full of wisdom and perfect in beauty.
> You were in Eden, the garden of God;
> Every precious stone *was* your covering:
> The sardius, topaz, and diamond,
> Beryl, onyx, and jasper,
> Sapphire, turquoise, and emerald with gold.
> The workmanship of your timbrels and pipes
> Was prepared for you on the day you were created.
> (Ezek. 28:12–13 NKJV)

Describing him as "perfect in beauty" and referring to his presence in Eden makes it clear this passage is not about the king of Tyre but about Lucifer, who was decked out like royalty, adorned with "every precious stone," and given timbrels (small instruments like tambourines) and pipes (basically woodwind instruments). It makes sense that the angel in charge of worship in heaven included music as part of his domain and used it actively in his attempt to ascend to God's throne. In fact, when you list all the instruments mentioned in conjunction with Lucifer in Scripture, virtually all instrument families are represented: strings, percussion, and wind.

In case there's any doubt, the continuation of this same passage reinforces Lucifer's relationship with music. As the "guardian cherub" (Ezek. 28:14), Lucifer was anointed to lead with music. Through his "widespread trade" (Ezek. 28:16), he tried to exchange his role as worship leader with that of being the center of attention, the focus of worship. Once he was cast out of heaven to earth (Ezek. 28:17), he lost his job as worship leader but still retained his knowledge of the power of music and how to pervert it for his purposes.

> You were anointed as a guardian cherub,
>> for so I ordained you.
> You were on the holy mount of God;
>> you walked among the fiery stones.
> You were blameless in your ways
>> from the day you were created
>> till wickedness was found in you.
> Through your widespread trade
>> you were filled with violence,
>> and you sinned.
> So I drove you in disgrace from the mount of God,
>> and I expelled you, guardian cherub,
>> from among the fiery stones.
> Your heart became proud
>> on account of your beauty,
> and you corrupted your wisdom
>> because of your splendor.
> So I threw you to the earth;
>> I made a spectacle of you before kings.
>
> (Ezek. 28:14–17)

As much as I love music, I know the Enemy still likes to use it strategically to penetrate our minds and hearts with his ungodly message. Look at the way music has been intertwined with alcoholism, drug addiction, sexual promiscuity, self-destruction, and suicide in recent generations. Songs like the Rolling Stones "Sympathy for the Devil" in the late sixties, Foreigner's "Feels Like the First Time" in the seventies, and Ozzy Osbourne's "Suicide Solution" in the early eighties weren't exactly offering messages of hope.

If Lucifer is no longer in charge of worship in God's kingdom, then who is his replacement? We are! Christians are the Devil's replacement in this role of worship leader—yet another reason why he hates you and me so much. He lost his job to us.

God created us with the same three types of musical sound—strings (vocal cords), percussion (clapping), and wind (singing)—so we can be living instruments of worship. Throughout the psalms, we're instructed to praise him with our voices, our clapping, and our very breath. This reinforces once again that the greatest test of our lives will be who and

> The Christian life can be distilled down to our daily struggle over what and how to worship.

what we worship. The Enemy wants us to worship anything other than God—to walk in his footsteps of unholy worship, whether it's bowing before him and what he portrays as worthy of praise, or giving in to cultural pressure and bowing before something else that seems like it should be elevated—like gold.

The Christian life can be distilled down to our daily struggle over what and how to worship. Open yourself up to what God might be trying to say to you about this. What is the Holy Spirit whispering to your heart?

The Firing Line

If you should doubt the truth that worship is our most basic struggle, just consider that the whole Bible begins and ends with a battle over worship. From tempting Eve and Adam in Genesis to dominating the world in Revelation, Satan has always wanted to turn people's worship—preferably to himself, but anything other than God will do. His sole purpose is to force good people to bow to cultural idols that are not worthy.

We see the beginnings of forced worship in our culture today with the moral war already raging here in America. It wasn't enough that abortion was legalized; now we're being forced to offer it and pay for it via support systems in our workplaces. There are numerous battles of belief, and you may find yourself in the midst of one right now. From redefining the institution of marriage to determining who uses which public restrooms, our culture is repeatedly forcing us to comply with standards that directly violate our Christian faith.

Rather than continue to list these various battles, I'd rather cut to the chase and consider how we should respond to any such confrontation. After considering the blatant coercion Daniel faced, let's see how he and his Hebrew friends stood their ground rather than bow before the king's idol.

> Shadrach, Meshach and Abednego replied to the king, "King Nebuchadnezzar, we do not need to defend ourselves before you in this matter. If we are thrown into the blazing furnace, the God we serve is able to save us from it, and he will rescue us from Your Majesty's hand. But even if he does not, we want you to know, Your Majesty, that we will not serve your gods or worship the image of gold you have set up." (Dan. 3:16–18)

Talk about staying cool while facing the firing line! Notice they didn't lead a rebellion, plan a boycott, condemn the king for building his idol, or argue about why they shouldn't have to bow down. In fact, they told the king they didn't need to defend their decision in this matter. They simply said, "We will not bow." They made it clear they trusted the Lord to rescue them—and here's the key to their stand: even if he didn't, they still would not regret their decision. In the end, they were cast into the furnace, yet none of them received the slightest scorch mark. God protected them and honored their fireproof faith.

Where did they get this kind of resolve? As we've seen, they definitely had the right foundation. They knew who they were despite the Babylonians' attempt to mock their identities. They had settled what they believed before they were taken captive. And they embraced the opportunity to strengthen their faith by courageously enduring the trials set before them. These three pillars—believe, embrace, and endure—support the kind of character needed to take a stand in a way that isn't defensive or combative.

You Are What You Worship

Sometimes, though, the idols in our lives aren't as clear as a large golden statue, or even today's cultural lifting up of self over God's original intents. But the truth is, we all worship something, whether we're deliberate about it or not. We all bow to something. Every day, all day long, and everywhere we go, we worship. It's what we do, and it's who we are. Worship is our response to what we value most. Often, whether unconsciously or consciously, we allow culture to determine what it is that we value most.

> Worship is our response to what we value most.

How do you know where and what you worship? Just follow the trail of your time, affection, energy, money, and loyalty. They will lead you to the truth about what you worship.

We all need to think through and identify what we're really worshipping. Everybody has an altar. We may not have it set up in our homes like a pagan shrine, but what we value most in life will always have the place of greatest prominence.

We are the only part of creation that does this—that offers up our worship. Why? Because we are created in God's image, created to bring pleasure and glory to the One who made us. But not all of us choose to worship God—and if you're not worshipping him, I promise you, you're still worshipping something. It's like breathing; it's how you're made.

But you'll never be satisfied, empowered for your purpose, or fulfilled in life as long as you worship anything other than God. So many have clearly exchanged the Creator for something he created as the center of their lives. This is exactly what the Devil wants—to have us derailed and in the ditches, away from God and away from who he created us to be.

Christians do it as well as nonbelievers, arousing the jealousy of our God as we bend to the innumerable things the world convinces us are the most important. When we attach ourselves to anything other than God for ultimate meaning in our lives, it's idolatry. It can be something we're addicted to—prescription pills, illegal drugs, alcohol, porn, sex, shopping, or gambling. It can be something that's a positive by itself, such as our family or work or even church. But if we elevate it to the most important thing in our lives above God, it's still idolatry.

> You'll never be satisfied, empowered for your purpose, or fulfilled in life as long as you worship anything other than God.

Unholy Trinity

I'm convinced idolatry runs rampant in our culture today. Simply consider what most people spend their money on—and perhaps more important, what they aspire to: more money, bigger houses, more possessions, fitter bodies, more power. Although the Bible is quite clear on the subject of idolatry, some people dismiss it as no longer being applicable, because "that's the Old Testament." But that's simply not true; the New Testament could not be clearer: "Therefore, my dear friends, flee from idolatry" (1 Cor. 10:14).

Throughout the Bible three false gods are mentioned repeatedly. There's the spirit of mammon, the god of possessions and greed. His worshippers' motto could have been "never enough." The same mind-set manifests itself today in the way many people pursue riches, assuming this will make them happy. Mammon always tries to squeeze into our hearts in place of God (Matt. 6:4). It's okay to have money—as long as money doesn't have you.

The next is Baal, a god of power and the root of all pride (Judg. 2:11, 10:10; 1 Kings 18:18; Jer. 2:23; Hos. 2:17). He's all about self-achievement and self-sufficiency. Remember those crazy fun-house mirrors (or now the apps) that make you look like a circus strongman? Baal basically reflects this kind of image back at his worshippers, saying, "You don't need God! You're strong enough to control it all yourself."

We see this same attitude today in the way we assume we can control our lives if we stay busy. It's the driving force behind workaholism and our out-of-control schedules. We drive too fast because we feel like we're perpetually late and must catch up any way we can. We eat in our cars while returning calls and scanning e-mails and texts. At work we're thinking we need to be at home, and at home we're thinking we need to be at work. So many of us spend minutes a day with our children and spouses, even less time with God, and work nine or ten hour days, which illustrates the spirit of Baal is alive and well in the twenty-first century!

Finally, there's Asherah, the goddess of pleasure—specifically sensual pleasures of the flesh (1 Kings 14:23; 2 Kings 17:10; Jer. 7:16–18). Sometimes called Ashtoreth as well, this goddess intensifies lustful appetites and worships through sexual acts. This idol has been around for centuries, including Venus for the ancient Romans and Aphrodite for the Greeks, and focuses on fertility. Worshippers live by the credo "if it feels good, do it!"

I think you'll agree that this god of sensual pleasure, lust, and sexual fulfillment has many modern worshippers. I don't need to cite the latest statistics about rape, human trafficking, and pornography to make a case. Not to mention the no-holds-barred mind-set regarding homosexuality and pretty much all forms of sexual expression. And we're not just talking about men here. Even suburban soccer moms worship Asherah, accounting for most of the 125 million copies of *Fifty Shades of Grey* sold worldwide (through June 2015).[1]

These false gods—power, money, and sex—have been warring against our relationship with the living God from the beginning. They popped up in the garden of Eden: "When the woman saw that the fruit of the tree was *good for food* and *pleasing to the eye*, and also *desirable for gaining wisdom*, she took some and ate it. She also gave some to her husband, who was with her, and he ate it" (Gen.

> These false gods—power, money, and sex—have been warring against our relationship with the living God from the beginning.

3:6, emphasis mine). Here we have mammon's greed ("good for food"), Asherah's appeal to pleasure ("pleasing to the eye"), and Baal's emphasis on self-empowerment ("desirable for gaining wisdom").

We also see these same three counterfeit gods used when the Devil tempted Jesus right after his forty-day fast in the desert:

The tempter came to him and said, "If you are the Son of God, *tell these stones to become bread*." . . .

Then the devil took him to the holy city and had him stand on the highest point of the temple. "If you are the Son of God," he said, "*throw yourself down*." . . .

Again, the devil took him to a very high mountain and showed him all the kingdoms of the world and their splendor. "*All this I will give you*," he said, "if you will bow down and worship me." (Matt. 4:3, 5–6, 8–9, emphasis mine)

Appealing to Jesus' hunger after his fast, the Devil attempts an appetite-fueled temptation to "turn stones into bread" (Asherah), followed by the encouragement to show off his power and "throw yourself down" (Baal), and finally the promise of "all this I will give you" (Mammon). By appealing to human appetites and senses, our pride, and our greed, these false gods remain powerful tools of our Enemy. It is likely these same three will confront you in some form of temptation today.

Nebuchadnezzar featured them as well in the temptations he offered in Daniel 3. The king's statue was dramatic in appearance, made of gold and ninety feet tall. It represented the power of the king and his pride. And it was accompanied by sensual music to complete the worship trifecta. As has been the case from the beginning of creation, the battle will always be over our hearts and what we worship.

We face this battle right now, today, over who gets our worship. Like Daniel and his friends, we are pressured to bow down on a daily basis. We must take a stand and be willing to say, "I am not going to bow to Hollywood's images. I will not support my government's demands to compromise my faith. I will not yield to my fleshly desires to make myself and my pleasure the center of my life."

Today we will worship the living God, our Lord and Savior, Jesus Christ.

Today we see our line in the sand.

And we will not cross it.

Five

WHEN THEY SAY I CAN'T

If we ever forget that we are one nation under God, then we will be a nation gone under.

—RONALD REAGAN

I t's cancer."

I stared at my phone screen and reread my sister Karol's text over and over again. She had accompanied Dad to his doctor's appointment earlier and had promised to let me know how it went. I had just pulled into the church parking lot and was about to return to my office when I saw her text. Gasping as if I'd been tackled by a lineman, I doubled over against the hood of my car. The fear that had been lurking in the back of my mind now fully surfaced and was becoming reality. My father had cancer.

It wasn't just that I loved my dad; he was my hero, my friend, my mentor in the Christian faith. He had been the best man at my wedding, and as Church of the Highlands began to grow, my dad had moved from Baton Rouge to Birmingham to help us. He was deeply intertwined in every aspect of my life, and I couldn't imagine any of it without him.

Walking into church on autopilot, I went up to my office and shut the door. I slumped into the chair behind my desk and began wrestling with feelings I couldn't even name. As a pastor and a student of God's Word for decades, I had all the biblical answers and pastoral training for situations like this. I knew God's truth. I believed God's truth. None of that changed. But suddenly I didn't know what to do. Just as Daniel had been a captive of the Babylonians, I felt as though I was suddenly being held hostage by heavy emotions I couldn't process.

So, feeling desperate for God, I did the only thing I knew to do: I turned on some praise and worship music. That probably sounds strange. Worship and grief don't usually go hand in hand. But I'd learned to practice worshipping God no matter what circumstances I faced, and that day wouldn't be any different. God promises us peace that surpasses all understanding in Philippians 4:7. But don't miss the instruction attached to this blessing. Philippians 4:4 is the key that unlocks this peace: "Rejoice in the Lord always. I will say it again: Rejoice!" Worship didn't erase my grief in the moment, but it definitely turned up an overriding peace. A peace I couldn't have found any other way.

I let the goodness of who God is soothe me. I felt his power strengthen me. I sensed his presence as he comforted me. And though I knew I would grieve over Dad's cancer again and again, I also took comfort in the reality that I could survive this news.

My dad's death would not be the death of the best parts of me. His influence would forever live on through me. The hallmark of his last days wouldn't be grief but rather the fullness of life. During this season, while my father battled for his life, God gave me a verse to focus on: "The Lord will rescue me from every evil attack and will bring me safely to his heavenly kingdom" (2 Tim. 4:18). As I reflected on the meaning of this verse, I thought, *Well, which is it? Will God rescue my dad from this evil attack? Or will Dad go safely into heaven?*

Eventually, I realized the answer was "yes"—and both happened. After his initial treatment and chemo successfully eradicated the disease from his body, the cancer returned the following year, and my beloved father passed away a few months later. I grieved then, and I still miss him. But it brings me great joy knowing where Dad is right now and that I'll get to see him again someday. With God, we're always in a win-win situation. No matter what's at risk or what we lose—even the most precious people in our lives—God's goodness will sustain us.

But the pivotal moment in the whole journey of Dad's illness was that day in my office—the day I worshipped God and refused to bow to fear, pain, and despair. All of hell wants us to bow to anything other than God. It may be the most important decision we'll make in the cultural shift: who we will and will not worship. If I had chosen not to worship at that time, the world would have understood. After all, death and sickness are universally known to take people out for at least a little

> Through worship, we move from viewing our problems as big and God as small to the exact opposite: because we remember how big our God is.

while. Choosing to worship in the midst of all this—that might have been the last course of action most would think of or recommend. But then, doesn't stepping out in faith usually run counter to the logic of this world?

Getting the news of Dad's diagnosis that day was like my lions' den moment, because my mind told me that God had abandoned me—cancer felt more powerful than God. But rather than give in to the despair of looming circumstances, I chose to worship no matter what and never bow to the pressures of life. And you can do that too. Worship changes everything. Through worship, we move from viewing our problems as big and God as small to the exact opposite: because we remember how big our God is.

Worship restores our perspective.

Warning Signs

Personal crises and painful circumstances aren't the only obstacles that we must battle with prayer and praise. Anytime we face a crossroads moment and cultural calamity sends us reeling, we must hold to our core convictions and never take our eyes off Jesus, even if—and perhaps especially when—the world pressures us to do just that.

Values that traditionally have been held high are under attack from all sides today. The institution of marriage has been re-defined. Our schools cater to contrarian special interests instead of biblical truth. Our leaders condone and approve of taking the lives of our unborn children. Cracks continue to spread across the moral foundation of our nation, shattering biblical beliefs—not to mention commonsense values—once considered so important. Many people believe one major blow occurred in 1962 when the Supreme Court ruled that prayer had to be taken out of public schools.

If you're under fifty years old, you probably can't even imagine our country including prayer in its classrooms. But in fact, before this ruling most school days began with the Pledge of Allegiance followed by a prayer like this: "Almighty God, we acknowl-edge our dependence on Thee and we beg Thy blessing over us, our parents, our teachers, and our nation." Eventually, though, enough people were offended by this that the highest court in our land decreed that prayer must go.

This may not seem to be such a big deal, especially consid-ering what we've grown accustomed to these days, but there are always unforeseen consequences when we bend to public opinion and remove God and the perspective that comes from regularly communing with him. It's not a slippery slope—it's one domino toppling the next until all Christian values have been leveled. Consider all that's happened since prayer was removed.

Teenage pregnancy rates went up 500 percent after 1962. The number of unmarried mothers also rose dramatically. The divorce rate is now so high that many young children don't even understand what a family looks like. Violent crimes have risen steadily since the early sixties, and our prison system is now bursting at the seams.[1]

Another way to look at it is to consider the decline in educational performance. After 1962, SAT scores declined steadily each year for almost two decades before reaching a plateau, one that has now started to decline again. We once had the best school system in the world, but now we're ranked about fifteenth among industrialized countries—this despite spending more money on our school system than any other nation in the world.[2]

It's an astonishing shift, to say the least. I'm not proposing that we put prayer back in schools. Today such a move would require every other belief system be allowed to do the same. I simply want to point out how quickly moral compromises can erode our society. We've gone from a decree that prayer has no place in public schools to rulings like the one in New Mexico in August 2013, which declared that sexual freedom trumps religious freedom. In this case the State Supreme Court ruled that a Christian photographer cannot decline to take pictures of a same-sex couple's commitment ceremony, despite the fact that doing so would violate his faith convictions.[3]

We've come a long way, and our downward slide continues. Things were far from perfect in past decades, but there was a safety net of shared moral values beneath us. There was the freedom to worship God that our ancestors fought so passionately to achieve.

Today, however, I'm afraid that safety net, that freedom, has been ripped to shreds and woven into a snare set by our Enemy.

Then and Now

Similarities between what Daniel experienced while captive in Babylon and what Christians face today are unmistakable. At least four parallels seem to be mirror images of one another. Let's briefly consider each one:

1. *We live in a society hostile to faith in God.* Daniel faced a pagan culture with no interest in, respect for, or fear of the living God. The Babylonians tried to force Daniel and his fellow Jews to relinquish their faith and embrace the cultural customs of their captors. While Christians in our country face cultural peer pressure, we must remember our brothers and sisters in other countries who on a daily basis face severe and dramatic persecution for their faith. As we're instructed in Scripture (1 Peter 5:9), stand firm and pray for those who are suffering and being martyred right now.

2. *We face commands from those in authority to do something that violates the essence of our faith.* The Babylonian kings ordered Daniel and their other Hebrew prisoners to worship pagan idols or face death. They consistently worked to eliminate Daniel's faith in God and replace it with cultural conformity based on political pressure and deadly enforcement. Now consider the Supreme Court battle Hobby Lobby fought in response to the Health Care Reform Act, which forced them to subscribe to a healthcare plan that would provide the morning-after pill for their employees. The court ruled in Hobby Lobby's favor in the end and

they won the case, but similar legal battles still loom on the horizon.

3. *We face serious consequences for noncompliance.* Daniel and other Jews remained imprisoned and faced trial after trial as the Babylonians attempted to assimilate them. The Hebrew captives likely faced physical punishment and torture as well as several life-threatening encounters with furnaces and lions. Our consequences may not be as immediate or seem as dangerous, but they are none-theless punitive. Currently, one of our time's biggest moral debates is about how churches should respond to homosexual marriage. If we don't perform ceremonies for homosexual couples, will the government take away our tax-exempt status? But then, who says we have to conduct state marriages? We answer to God—not the mayor, gov-ernor, or president. Will our ministries serving those who are in need be crippled by the consequences of standing firm on what the Bible says about marriage?

4. *We endure cultural and societal punishment for maintain-ing our beliefs.* Considering the life of Daniel, we realize just how extraordinary he was—not only to survive his Babylonian captors' trials and tortures but to influence them with his steadfast faith. Daniel never allowed his fear, anxiety, or concerns to impede his faith or inhibit his obe-dience to God. Today, we must look to his example for the strength and courage to do the same, because we will face serious consequences when we stand firm in whom and how we worship. Some have lost their jobs, their elected offices, their businesses, and their reputations. Some have sat in courtrooms and jail cells, refusing to compromise their bedrock faith in God and his ways.

These similarities reflect the advancement of what I call the anti-Christ spirit of our age: the persecution of Christianity, the Bible, churches, and Christian values by means of coercion, authoritative control, and cultural consequences of condemnation. The Bible warns us:

> The coming of the lawless one will be in accordance with how Satan works. He will use all sorts of displays of power through signs and wonders that serve the lie, and all the ways that wickedness deceives those who are perishing. They perish because they refused to love the truth and so be saved. For this reason God sends them a powerful delusion so that they will believe the lie and so that all will be condemned who have not believed the truth but have delighted in wickedness. (2 Thess. 2:9–12)

These four parallels between Daniel's Babylon and the world around us are no coincidence. There's more going on than what we can see on the surface. The spirit of the Antichrist that was at work in Daniel's day continues today in his mission of overthrowing God and destroying God's followers. Typically, it's a two-pronged attack. First, the Enemy tries to get people to exalt humans above God. Second, he attempts to stop the worship of God. We see both strategies pervading our culture.

Perhaps the easiest way to get us to elevate humanity above God is to make life all about us. The Devil executes his plan by working nonstop to replace God's truth with two big lies: (1) "If it feels good, do it!" and (2) "Live your own truth—do what is right for you." Our spiritual Enemy has all kinds of cultural weapons at his disposal to promote this kind of a mind-set that places our own desires over all else. Business, sports, entertainment, money, power, fame, pleasure, sex—they're all enticements that can shift the focus from God to us if we elevate them to become our top priorities.

The Devil knows that if he can get us entirely dependent on something earthly, then we'll be miserable and will only want more and more of it to escape our pain. The paradoxical cycle of addiction is a deathtrap for so many people. But what's worse is when this paves the way for the suppression of people of faith who have not chosen to participate. And we see the early signs of this already, of our religious freedom being limited by cultural whims.

Issues such as legalized abortion—not only allowing it but forcing taxpayers to pay for it—and homosexual marriage have ripped the moral fabric of our nation. We now face forced compliance with acts that go against our faith. And we must be prepared to trust God and face the consequences—whatever those may be. Culture loves to drive a wedge between our convictions and our worship. If the world can force us to abandon God's truth, then it can push us toward worshipping its idols and not our holy God.

Worship is respecting who God is and how he sees things. It's acknowledging that he is God and we are his creation. The clarions of culture want to force us to abandon our form of worship because they find it offensive. Because our ongoing, faithful obedience to God and his Word threatens those who want to undermine God's existence and his role in our lives.

> Culture loves to drive a wedge between our convictions and our worship.

And so our culture consistently and continually tries to erode the truth about God and place his power in human hands.

But our religious freedom is foundational to our country's existence—this is why the Pilgrims left their homes behind, sailed perilous waters, and started over in the dangerous wilderness they discovered after landing at Plymouth Rock. These early pioneers of the faith knew what we must now remember. Likewise, as Peter and the apostles explained to the Jewish religious leaders trying to arrest them for preaching the gospel of Christ, "We must obey God rather than human beings!" (Acts 5:29).

An Uncompromising Position

There can be no doubt: biblical values are slipping away. With that erosion, so, too, our religious freedoms begin to shrink. As culture shifts, new limitations emerge in an attempt to determine what we can and cannot do. The world now does not want us to worship God the way we choose. Basically, our situation is no different from the conflict Daniel faced in Babylon.

After facing cultural challenges and surviving a fiery test of faith, Daniel had to endure his greatest culture clash yet. After Nebuchadnezzar, Babylon was ruled by a new leader, Darius. Although Daniel continued to maintain a place of influence in the royal court, many officials remained jealous that this Hebrew outsider held power within their midst. So they plotted to kill Daniel and get rid of him once and for all.

> Finally these men said, "We will never find any basis for charges against this man Daniel unless it has something to do with the law of his God."
>
> So the administrators and the satraps went as a group to the king and said: "May King Darius live forever! The royal administrators, prefects, satraps, advisers and governors have all agreed that the king should issue an edict and enforce the decree that anyone who prays to any god or man during the next thirty days, except to you, Your Majesty, shall be thrown into the lions' den. Now, Your Majesty, issue the decree and put it in writing so that it cannot be altered—in accordance with the laws of the Medes and Persians, which cannot be repealed." So King Darius put the decree in writing. (Dan. 6:5–9)

Having failed at forcing Daniel to worship something other than God, the Babylonians now wanted to prevent him from worshipping his God at all. They devised a clever plan to force Daniel's hand—from a position of prayer and worship to the living God to one of full submission to their king. But notice, once again, how Daniel responded:

> Now when Daniel learned that the decree had been published, he went home to his upstairs room where the windows opened toward Jerusalem. Three times a day he got down on his knees and prayed, giving thanks to his God, just as he had done before. Then these men went as a group and found Daniel praying and asking God for help. So they went to the king and spoke to him about his royal decree: "Did you not publish a decree that during the next thirty days anyone who prays to any god or man except to you, Your Majesty, would be thrown into the lions' den?" The king answered, "The decree stands—in accordance with the laws of the Medes and Persians, which cannot be repealed." (Dan. 6:10–12)

What did Daniel do in the face of this royal decree? He prayed! He worshipped God and prayed three times a day—"just as he had done before." Daniel didn't panic, he didn't force a confrontation, and he didn't argue about the unfairness of the decree. He simply did what he had always done—prayed and worshipped the Lord he loved and served.

Are we willing to make the same commitment? Will we resolve that no matter what happens or who tries to influence us that we will not bow before any other god? That we will continue to worship only God? Do we have the kind of courage Daniel had?

The Fruit of Courage

Daniel consistently refused to give in to the demands of his captors and their culture. He would not bow down to their idols or participate in their unhealthy hedonism. And when they told him he could not pray to anyone but the king, he didn't even blink. He went home and prayed three times as usual. His example continues to be a witness to the world; the way we handle cultural pressure always is. As we touched on in chapter 3, to walk in Daniel's footsteps, we must have courage. But more than courage, we must demonstrate the fruit of courage—action.

Courage was certainly something we saw in the lives of Jesus' disciples, especially after he had returned to heaven and sent them the Holy Spirit. It's even mentioned in a number of scenes: "When they saw the *courage* of Peter and John and realized that they were unschooled, ordinary men, they were astonished and they took note that these men had been with Jesus" (Acts 4:13, emphasis mine). The public officials threatened to kill the disciples because of their beliefs and teaching, yet they stood fearlessly in the face of this threat.

This kind of courage got the attention of the people, who then noticed that the disciples were not men of intellect with considerable religious training. They were just ordinary fishermen. But they had spent time with Jesus, which had left an indelible mark on them, fueling limitless reserves of courage for all they would face.

We see the fruit of the disciples' courage later in the same chapter (Acts 4) when they attend a prayer meeting: "After they prayed, the place where they were meeting was shaken. And they were all filled with the Holy Spirit and spoke the word of God *boldly*" (v. 31, emphasis mine).

This boldness is what I want for you—and for all of us who

follow Jesus and want to stand strong in our bow-down culture: The boldness to stand courageously in the face of an ever-shifting culture. To speak up even when what you believe isn't popular. It may not feel good—but the rewards are eternal. We're told, "Do not lose your courage, then, because it brings with it a great reward" (Heb. 10:35 GNT). And, as we've seen with the disciples, the key to courage always comes back to spending time with Jesus. The more time we spend with Jesus, the more courage we will have.

> The key to courage always comes back to spending time with Jesus.

This kind of courage is not reserved for pillars of the faith like Daniel, David, Paul, and the other disciples. It's available to you and me. If you look at strong people of faith, I believe you will find in them tried and tested, fireproof, lion-proof faith. These people have as many problems as anyone else, but they also have something else: the promises of God and his Word, and the courage to act on them.

When I pray each day, I always read God's Word first. Then I ask the Lord to illuminate a verse or an idea from what I've just read. And then I listen. In fact, a long time ago I learned to always keep pen and paper close by when I pray. Some of the best, most creative ideas have come to me when I pray and listen to God as he speaks to my heart through Scripture.

This kind of personal word from the Lord is a promise deep down inside us. Without it, we'll be tempted to panic and cave under the pressure when the going gets tough. Despite the storm swirling around us, a word from God gives us the assurance to stand tall and to speak boldly. This is one of the main reasons I encourage you to spend time every day reading God's Word and reflecting on it in prayer. And whether you understand it or not, whether you like it or not, accept its authority.

Even when I don't like it, God's Word tells me the truth. Sometimes it makes me miserable as it confronts areas of my heart and life that need to change. But if I submit myself to God's truth, it sets me free. Surrendering to God's truth strengthens our convictions and fuels our courage, providing confidence in the face of the storm.

> These words I speak to you are not incidental additions to your life, homeowner improvements to your standard of living. They are foundational words, words to build a life on. If you work these words into your life, you are like a smart carpenter who built his house on solid rock. (Matt. 7:24 MSG)

If we build our lives on popular opinion or our feelings, then we will always feel unstable and insecure, fearful that everything could change at any moment. Without the certainty of God's character and his Word, life has no stable foundation. But when we rely on him, we will enjoy the peace of mind and fullness of heart that comes from knowing that God's got this. He's the same yesterday, today, and forever. He loves us, and nothing can change that.

Speak Up

Daniel wasn't the first to risk everything and trust God with the outcome. Abraham was asked to sacrifice his precious son, Isaac, the miracle child he and Sarah had been promised and had waited for and finally conceived in their old age. Why would God give them this amazing gift only to ask them to give it back? Only God knew. But Abraham wasn't asked to understand God's logic or motive; Abraham was simply asked to obey.

By faith Abraham, when God tested him, offered Isaac as a sacrifice. He who had embraced the promises was about to sacrifice his one and only son, even though God had said to him, "It is through Isaac that your offspring will be reckoned." Abraham reasoned that God could even raise the dead, and so in a manner of speaking he did receive Isaac back from death. (Heb. 11:17–19)

Abraham reasoned that God could raise the dead. He trusted the Lord to do the seemingly impossible because Abraham had already seen God do it before. Abraham didn't refuse despite how unimaginable the sacrifice. You see, courage doesn't try to figure out all the answers

> Courage looks up, stands up, and speaks up.

and refuse to act until it understands. Courage comes from the heart. Like love, courage requires a commitment of unbreakable trust. Courage is doing what you are afraid to do, and not allowing fear to rule your decisions. Simply put, courage looks up, stands up, and speaks up.

As Christians, many of us have a hard time speaking up for Jesus in public. Again, this struggle is nothing new: the apostle John tells us that even when Jesus walked among them, "No one had the courage to speak favorably about [Jesus] in public" (John 7:13 NLT). But the need to speak up in the name of Christ has never been greater.

I'm sure many of us have thought, *I don't know what to say that won't hurt people. I don't know how to reach them. My Christian views will seem so unloving—others won't understand. If I stand for truth, what will people think of me?*

But this is a risk we have to take. If we keep our hearts purely focused through continual prayer and praise and season our words with God's grace, then we don't have to worry about what others may think. God's truth has the power to set people free—this should fuel our desire to connect with others, not a smug attempt to prove we're right.

We know some people won't want to hear what we have to say. Others may not like what we say, but they will respect us for speaking up and see our motive is not to be right but to be loving. This can be challenging, because, as I said in chapter 2, it's easy to slip into an "us vs. them" attitude in which grace evaporates. But this can be averted by daily coming into God's presence and aligning our perspectives with his. Then we will be strengthened both in the love with which we approach people and in our boldness and courage to engage rather than shy away from the conversation.

> God's truth has the power to set people free—this should fuel our desire to connect with others, not a smug attempt to prove we're right.

We all need to be encouraged in this. Even the great apostle Paul needed encouragement in this area: "One night the Lord spoke to Paul in a vision: 'Do not be afraid; keep on speaking, do not be silent'" (Acts 18:9).

"Wait a minute, Chris," you might be saying. "What's the big deal? I don't need to speak up as long as I'm right with God in my heart." And I would answer you by directing you to what Jesus said: "Stand up for me against world opinion and I'll stand up for you before my Father in heaven" (Matt. 10:32 MSG).

And if we don't? The next verse explains the consequences: "But everyone who denies me here on earth, I will also deny before my Father in heaven" (Matt. 10:33 NLT).

Do you realize how important it is that you not be a coward

about your faith? Jesus said essentially, "Hey, if you deny me here on earth, I will deny you before my Father in heaven. If you're ashamed of me, I'll be ashamed of you." Sound harsh? Not if you're seriously committed to what you believe.

Consider how vocal everyone else in the world is about their beliefs. As social media continues to give almost everyone access to a channel for expressing their opinions, people make it clear they're loud and proud of their viewpoints, but those with God's truth fear being misunderstood or hated. Christians remain timid, even reluctant, to speak up for fear of a lions' den looming ahead. But when these moments come up, think about Daniel, on his knees, praying as usual, despite the royal decree. Take courage, my friend, and stand strong in God's truth.

Refuse to give up your ground.

Do what God wants, not what people want.

Six ————————————————————————

WHEN THEY QUESTION
GOD'S RIGHT TO BE GOD

Faith is deliberate confidence in the character of God
whose ways you may not understand at the time.

—OSWALD CHAMBERS

I t was a spectacular sight. Purple balloons and gold streamers,
homemade signs, and banners draped entire neighborhoods—on
trees, mailboxes, sign posts, and yards—throughout the entire
city of Birmingham. But what made this so amazing wasn't just
that these were my beloved LSU Tigers' team colors; it was the
very personal catalyst behind this massive decorating spree.

Sid Ortis was a sixteen-year-old who loved his family, his God,
and, because his parents were from God's Country, also known as
Louisiana, his LSU Tigers. When Sid was diagnosed with bone
cancer, he fought a courageous battle through numerous surgeries
and chemotherapy treatments. Word spread quickly of his positive, faith-filled spirit.

To show support, neighbors and people throughout the city of
Birmingham blanketed every street and neighborhood with LSU's
colors. Keep in mind, Alabama is usually draped in other colors,
like crimson and white or blue and orange, especially during football season. We are serious about football here in Alabama, so this
change in color scheme was rather a big deal.

Even LSU's head football coach, Les Miles, heard about Sid's battle and reached out to the young man, calling to chat and pray and inviting him to be on the field for their upcoming game against Auburn, a day that Sid later described as "the best day ever!"

When Sid's body lost its battle against cancer, we were saddened for his family and for the amazing young man we had lost in our community. Yet we knew that his spirit lived on and that somehow, beyond the limitations of our understanding, God knew what he was doing. We would miss Sid terribly but took comfort in his passionate heart and fighting spirit.

I remember Sid's mother, Lynn, saying that she believed God was sparing Sid from something else that would have come along later in life had he lived. She said Sid was the only one of her children she worried would go wild and get into trouble. I shared a verse with her, one I also read at Sid's funeral: "Good people pass away; the godly often die before their time. . . . No one seems to understand that God is protecting them from the evil to come" (Isa. 57:1 NLT).

> God is still God even when we don't understand his ways.

So often nonbelievers in our culture refuse to believe in a God who would allow someone like Sid to suffer with cancer and die so young. They can't reconcile that a good God would allow the atrocities that they often see in our world today: natural disasters and calamitous events, birth defects and cancer, torture and genocide. But this is why our response, as Christians, to these events matters so much.

We may struggle with some of the same questions, doubts, and concerns in the face of such tragedies. But this is when we must exercise our faith to the fullest. This is when we must choose to worship God and to trust in his goodness, sovereignty, and power. This is when we remind the world around us that we are not God. And even if he's not being God the way we think he should, it doesn't matter. He's still God. We are the creation, not the Creator. God is still God even when we don't understand his ways.

Begging the Question

Being in the ministry means I pray for a lot of people who need a miracle from God—and it also means I've conducted a lot of funerals for many of those same people. While I never have a hard time trusting God's timing in taking them home—after all, heaven is better than Alabama—like most people I still wonder why God doesn't heal more sick people—especially ones like Sid who clearly had such a positive impact on those around him.

Don't get me wrong: I've seen God provide miraculous cures for late-stage cancer and give babies to couples struggling with infertility. I've seen people on the brink of death bounce back to full health without their doctors being able to explain it. God clearly grants miracles every day. But why doesn't he do it more? Why do some people get healed while others suffer and die? No matter how many miracles you see, these questions beg to be asked. It's just human nature.

But some things never make sense.

As Christians, we often succumb to playing the same mental games others do when a crisis happens or tragedy strikes. We ask, *Why did this have to happen? Why couldn't you have prevented this, Lord?* Then we allow our doubts, fears, and uncertainties to bounce around our minds like pinballs, cycling around and around without any answers or resolutions. But the book of Daniel—along with Job, Ezekiel, Ecclesiastes, Lamentations, and other passages in Scripture—reminds us again and again that our place is not to demand answers from God or to try and analyze life's losses like a math problem.

When the unimaginable happens, we have to stop thinking, analyzing, and problem solving and simply trust God. It's the same kind of trust we learned as children when we questioned our parents about why we had to get a shot, take medicine, or avoid sharp objects. At the time we couldn't understand—and may not have had the mental development to understand—why we had to endure something so painful or forgo something that looked appealing. We had to trust that what motivated our parents' decisions was our health, safety, and well-being. In the same way, we must trust our heavenly Father even when unbearably painful events come our way.

We are never to weigh our thoughts, logic, and rationalization against his. When we do, we're shifting the focus of our worship from God to ourselves. True worship happens when you don't understand and choose to trust God anyway, acknowledging his goodness, power, and sovereignty even amid situations that defy rational human explanation. We have to trust that God didn't get it wrong even when we can't figure it out.

We don't have to understand God's ways—which I'm so grateful for because, in this life, we won't. We simply can't. But we can choose to love him, worship him, and serve him no matter what happens. No matter whether others can't fathom why we continue worshipping a God who doesn't make sense to them. We don't know for sure, but

> True worship happens when you don't understand and choose to trust God anyway.

I'm guessing Daniel wondered why God allowed his people to be captured and enslaved by brutal pagans like the Babylonians.

Back at the beginning of Daniel's story, you'll recall how this whole ordeal started:

> In the third year of the reign of Jehoiakim king of Judah, Nebuchadnezzar king of Babylon came to Jerusalem and besieged it. *And the Lord delivered Jehoiakim king of Judah into his hand, along with some of the articles from the temple of God.* These he carried off to the temple of his god in Babylonia and put in the treasure house of his god. (Dan. 1:1–2, emphasis mine)

Perhaps as events unfolded, Daniel wondered why his captor's culture had to test his faith at every turn. Why did his three friends have to be thrown into a red-hot furnace? Why did he have to come face-to-face with a den of ravenous lions?

While Daniel wasn't immune to such questions, his bedrock faith in God clearly trumped any doubts he might have had. I'm convinced this kind of faith was one of the main reasons he was so successful in the face of a pagan culture. Simply put, he knew God. He knew who God was and clearly knew the Word of God and the Lord's promises of deliverance. But where did this kind of trust come from? How did Daniel develop this superstrong faith that empowered him to stare down any test, trial, or temptation the Babylonians threw at him?

And how can we have this same kind of faith today?

The Faith of Job

Before we enter the lions' den with Daniel, I want to explore the challenges another man of great faith experienced. Job's name has become synonymous with patience and long-suffering, but clearly his trust in God was stretched to the breaking point. Everything Job endured seemed beyond anything he could have imagined, predicted, or expected—especially in light of who he knew God to be.

So when nothing around him made sense, how did Job continue to walk by faith? Why did he refuse to give up on God despite losing everyone he loved and everything he had, including his health? Let's dig in to his story for clues about the source of Job's remarkable faith.

> In the land of Uz there lived a man whose name was Job. This man was blameless and upright; he feared God and shunned evil. He had seven sons and three daughters, and he owned seven thousand sheep, three thousand camels, five hundred yoke of oxen and five hundred donkeys, and had a large number of servants. He was the greatest man among all the people of the East. (Job 1:1–3)

Right out of the gate, we're told Job was a good man. He's described as "blameless and upright," a man who worshipped God and avoided evil. It's also hard to miss that Job was not only a good guy, but he was one rich dude. It's not always easy to find someone who has it all, literally, but Job seemed to have been that balanced person at the beginning of our story. But having so much also meant that Job had more to lose. Let's see how his life first started to unravel:

> One day when Job's sons and daughters were feasting and drinking wine at the oldest brother's house, a messenger came to Job and said, "The oxen were plowing and the donkeys were grazing nearby, and the Sabeans attacked and made off with them. They put the servants to the sword, and I am the only one who has escaped to tell you!"
>
> While he was still speaking, another messenger came and said, "The fire of God fell from the heavens and burned up the

sheep and the servants, and I am the only one who has escaped to tell you!"

While he was still speaking, another messenger came and said, "The Chaldeans formed three raiding parties and swept down on your camels and made off with them. They put the servants to the sword, and I am the only one who has escaped to tell you!"

While he was still speaking, yet another messenger came and said, "Your sons and daughters were feasting and drinking wine at the oldest brother's house, when suddenly a mighty wind swept in from the desert and struck the four corners of the house. It collapsed on them and they are dead, and I am the only one who has escaped to tell you!"

At this, Job got up and tore his robe and shaved his head. Then he fell to the ground in worship and said:

"Naked I came from my mother's womb,
     and naked I will depart.
The LORD gave and the LORD has taken away;
     may the name of the LORD be praised."

In all this, Job did not sin by charging God with wrongdoing.
(Job 1:13–22)

Can you imagine how devastating it must have been for Job to receive bad news, only to have it overshadowed by worse and then even worse news? Then he faced about the worst news a father can receive: the death of all his children at once. Still, in the midst of losing his wealth and his children, Job chose to worship. He did not blame God and instead praised him.

Job's wife, on the other hand, responded the way so many people in our culture respond to terrible events—with intense anger toward God. But the Christian response must be closer to Job's than his wife's. Even when she told him to "curse God and die" (Job 2:9), Job refused to abandon his faith despite the overwhelmingly painful suffering he faced.

But Job wasn't perfect. Though he never blamed God, later on Job did question God—with a little help from his friends—as we discover throughout the next thirty-five chapters. I find Job's doubts reassuring because even when we trust God we still must wrestle with heartache, with loss, with disappointment, and with the doubts that may accompany such painful emotions. But we would do well to keep in mind what happened when Job questioned God.

> Even when we trust God we still must wrestle with heartache, with loss, with disappointment, and with the doubts that may accompany such painful emotions.

After Job finally voiced all his doubts, God answered him out of a thunderous storm:

Then the LORD spoke to Job out of the storm. He said:

> "Who is this that obscures my plans
>   with words without knowledge?
> Brace yourself like a man;
>   I will question you,
>   and you shall answer me.
>
> Where were you when I laid the earth's foundation?
> Tell me, if you understand.
>
> Who marked off its dimensions? Surely you know!"
>
> (Job 38:1–5)

God had had enough of the human wisdom from Job and those around him. Basically, God said, "You want answers? Then let me ask you a question first."

> Have you comprehended the vast expanses of the earth?
>> Tell me, if you know all this.
> What is the way to the abode of light?
>> And where does darkness reside?
> Can you take them to their places?
>> Do you know the paths to their dwellings?
> Surely you know, for you were already born!
>> You have lived so many years!
>
> (Job 38:18–21)

Like a frustrated parent, God made his point. Job immediately got it and reached a conclusion we all need to reach just as much: "Then Job answered the LORD: 'I am unworthy—how can I reply to you? I put my hand over my mouth'" (Job 40:3–4). Job realized he could not come close to comparing himself worthy of knowing and understanding God's ways.

Omni-Beliefs

Job is one of the characters in the Bible most often held up as a shining example of how to remain faithful under pressure. As such, when we look at his story, we can often come away feeling far from his level of trust and belief in God. It's easy to become discouraged and dismiss his example as beyond our reach, but if we look a little closer at the foundation of the faith that enabled his response, we'll see that it's not quite as impossible as it first seems.

Job's response was built on three components. Together, these omni-beliefs illustrate the kind of humble faith we need if we are to stay firmly rooted in the face of the world's reasoning that we should leave God behind when life's trials feel unbearable. Let's consider each one and how it applies to our lives.

A belief that God is all-powerful. The theological term for God's all-powerfulness is *omnipotence,* and it conveys more than sheer strength—it's the ultimate power that is the source of all other power we see in our world. It's the belief that nothing is too difficult for God. Job said, "I know that you can do all things; no purpose of yours can be thwarted" (Job 42:2).

When we're faced with a hard situation, one of the best ways to respond is to believe God can make a way where we can't see one. This kind of revelation will change our lives as we exercise our faith, trusting and believing that despite how irrational, illogical, or impossible the situation seems, God is bigger and more powerful.

We see this kind of sold-out, whole-hearted faith in the life of Joseph. Betrayed by his brothers, sold into slavery in Egypt, falsely accused, and imprisoned, Joseph had every reason to abandon his faith because God wasn't intervening and rescuing him. Instead, Joseph remained faithful and continued to worship God and exercise his faith in ways that, like Daniel's, got noticed by those around him. After Pharaoh made Joseph second in command, after Joseph saved thousands—perhaps millions—of lives by trusting God and stockpiling food for the coming famine, after he confronted his brothers, whom he also saved, Joseph could say to them: "You intended to harm me, but God intended it for good to accomplish what is now being done, the saving of many lives" (Gen. 50:20).

My faith, probably like yours, has been tested as well. At times in my life, someone looking in from the outside might have said it would make more sense to abandon the trust I had in God, whose guiding hand seemed confusing at best or invisible at worst. When, looking through human eyes, it might have seemed smarter to take things into my own hands rather than continue to believe in and follow God. But the way I see it, I'd rather have hope in what an all-powerful God can do than certainty in what I am limited to do.

A belief that God is all-knowing. Omniscient is the theological term for "all-knowing," and it simply means God is smarter and wiser than we have the ability to comprehend or imagine. Job recognized the vast difference between himself and God: "You asked, 'Who is this that obscures my plans without knowledge?' Surely I spoke of things I did not understand, things too wonderful for me to know" (Job 42:3). His observation about God's ways being "too wonderful for me to know" captures the essence of faith: accepting what you don't understand.

> I'd rather have hope in what an all-powerful God can do than certainty in what I am limited to do.

When my dad died two years after his diagnosis, I couldn't understand why God chose to bring him home to heaven for his perfect healing rather than heal him here on earth so I could spend more time with him. But I've got to believe God is all-knowing and beyond my right to question. I have to accept the limitations of my knowledge and ability to understand God's ways. Then I can rest in the confidence of his wisdom, timing, and purpose. It's as God said: "This plan of mine is not what you would work out, neither are my thoughts the same as yours! For just as the heavens are higher than the earth, so are my ways higher than yours, and my thoughts than yours" (Isa. 55:8–9 TLB).

God knows things we don't know; we simply have to trust

him. We want a better now, but God offers a better place for the rest of our lives. Remember: God knows the end of your story. He is at work right now in ways you can't see—all for your ultimate good and his glory. Can you dare to believe this and trust him with whatever is weighing on you right now at this moment?

A belief that God is ever-present. Theologians might say "omnipresent." This means God transcends the limits of time and space as we know it. He can be present with each one of us at any time, no matter where we are; all we must do is draw near and choose to meet him. Job said, "My ears had heard of you but now my eyes have seen you" (Job 42:5). So many of us know God from a distance, but if we get close—really up close and personal—then we'll know him and his heart and come to truly trust him.

I saw this when Sid Ortis's family, and Sid himself, pressed in closer to God rather than pulling away during his excruciating illness. Though the world would have said this amount of pain and unexplained hardship should make them think twice about God's presence and goodness, Sid and his family held tighter to the truth of who God was. They discovered the comfort and peace of God being with them at all times and in all places. They learned personally that "those who know your name trust in you, for you, Lord, have never forsaken those who seek you" (Ps. 9:10).

Job also knew this kind of closeness with God and clung to him even as everything in his life fell apart. In the end of Job's story, he got back all he lost—in fact, he was given twice as much. This didn't compensate for losing his loved ones or for going through such a painful season of grieving. But Job trusted the Lord whether times were good or times were bad, whether he had a lot or a little, whether he felt happy or felt sad. This is the kind of faith required if we are to stand up against the cultural forces our Enemy uses to ensnare us. This is the kind of faith we see in Daniel. No matter what he faced, he never argued or complained about how bad things were going. He simply trusted God and kept doing what he knew to do: pray, worship, obey.

Limits and Longings

After studying the examples of people like Job and Daniel, I'm convinced real worship ultimately boils down to trust. It's the belief that God gets to be God and we don't. In fact, we don't even have the right to question God and his ways, including his Word. If we only believe what we like in the Bible but don't believe what we don't like, then it's not the Bible that we trust but ourselves.

> Real worship ultimately boils down to trust.

Clearly choosing what we believe and, thus, who we trust, is at the heart of standing strong in the face of an ungodly culture. If we don't recognize the distinction between our role as human beings—creations of God who are made in his image—and the character and power of God, then eventually our doubts may erode our faith. Cultural forces will encourage us to abandon our beliefs about God and his Word and instead embrace humanism—the belief that we control our own lives.

We must recognize our limits as human beings—and our longings. The two go hand in hand. When we experience God's love and acceptance, when we worship him and walk with him and follow him, then it becomes easier to surrender our attempts to control life. Knowing and worshipping God fulfills us and organically grows our trust with deeper roots—even when it's incredibly painful, illogical, and seemingly unbearable.

We see this truth in evidence at the end of Jesus' time on earth. After dining with his disciples for the last time before his death,

Jesus—who clearly knew what he was about to face—prayed to his Father nonetheless.

> Jesus went out as usual to the Mount of Olives, and his disciples followed him. On reaching the place, he said to them, "Pray that you will not fall into temptation." He withdrew about a stone's throw beyond them, knelt down and prayed, "Father, if you are willing, take this cup from me; yet not my will, but yours be done." An angel from heaven appeared to him and strengthened him. And being in anguish, he prayed more earnestly, and his sweat was like drops of blood falling to the ground. (Luke 22:39–44)

Here is Jesus, God's only Son, asking his Father to take away the cup that waited before him, the one that included a bitter betrayal by one of his closest followers, a humiliating arrest on trumped-up charges, a torturous beating, and the most painful death possible. No one would want to go through all that—apparently, not even Christ! Nonetheless, after making his request known, he prayed that God's will would be done, not his own. Jesus yielded his own ability to control events—of course, Jesus was not only man but also God—and surrendered his will to his Father's. He trusted God with all that he was about to face, knowing he wished to avoid it but accepting it for the sake of all people.

And notice what Jesus told his disciples to pray while he was praying a few feet away from them: "Pray that you will not fall into temptation" (Luke 22:40). Christ knew that his followers would be tempted to abandon their faith, to give up hope, and, in Peter's case, to deny even knowing Jesus. Our Savior knew that when people cannot understand why God allows certain events, they're also tempted to lose faith. The human mind tries to make a rational narrative for why God allows suffering, disease, violence, crime, and so many other terrible forces to operate in our world. But we know God gave us a choice: the free will to decide for ourselves whether we will worship and obey him—or something, or someone, else.

Even if you can't understand what God is doing, will you still choose to trust him? When life doesn't make sense—and your view of what God's doing or not doing doesn't make sense either—you must be deliberate about where you will focus your worship.

Because there will always be someone or something trying to derail your faith. Someone or something competing for your worship.

What's competing for your worship right now? What's causing you to shift from bowing before God to worshipping an idol? Maybe it's a painful event or devastating loss that causes you to question God's goodness, power, and sovereignty. Perhaps because you can't understand certain situations and challenging relationships in your life, you're tempted to back away from God and pour yourself into something else.

> The Enemy doesn't come dressed in a red jumpsuit, wearing little horns. He comes dressed in everything we think we want.

Maybe your career is getting your worship—devotion to working hard, impressing others, and getting a promotion. There's nothing wrong with enjoying your career and being committed to excellence. But if it's what you prize above all else—because that's how you feel valued and affirmed—then it's an idol.

Maybe sports take up too much of your time. Attending a football game, your kid's soccer match, or any such event you feel passionately about can seem like a religious experience. There's focus, devotion, music, celebration, even lament for the losing team's fans. But when taken to an extreme, sports can become a poor substitute for knowing the living God.

Nothing will satisfy us like worshipping God. That's why the Devil works so hard to redirect our worship to anything else. And in the process he takes the credit and enjoys being worshipped as well. The Enemy doesn't come dressed in a red jumpsuit, wearing little horns. He comes dressed in everything we think we want.

So we must be careful what we choose.

We always become what we worship.

If you don't like who you're becoming, then take an inventory of what you store in your heart. If you don't like what you find, then simply ask God to forgive you and restore his place on the throne of your heart.

If you haven't surrendered yourself to Jesus and bowed your heart in worship, or if you've allowed something else to take his place, then I must ask you these questions: Isn't it time? Isn't now the time to fulfill that longing in the deepest part of your being and encounter the God who made you, knows you, and loves you? Isn't it about time to bow down to Jesus?

When I gave my heart to Christ, I didn't know what to pray. I didn't have the words. Someone helped me say what I wanted to say, like a preacher does at a wedding when the bride and groom recite their vows after him. It's really not difficult at all. The Bible tells us, if we want to be saved, we have to declare Jesus as

> We always become what we worship.

our Lord with our mouths—then believe in our hearts that he is God. Then we are saved (Rom. 10:9–10).

Now is the time to stop reading this book and take a moment to pray. Here's a little prayer in case you need help with the words. Feel free to make them your own. And most important, mean what you pray.

Dear God, I need you. I need a real relationship with you. Today I open my life to knowing you. Forgive me for living my life my way. Today I invite Jesus to be the Lord of my life. Jesus, I want to know you. I put my trust in you, for the things I understand and for the things I don't understand. Today I declare that you are all-powerful, all-knowing, and always present. You are my God. In your name I pray, amen.

Part 3

Culture's Greatest Question: Who Is in Charge of My Life?

Who Is in Control—Me or God?

Seven ————————————————————————————————

END-TIMES INSANITY

What makes humility so desirable is the marvelous
thing it does to us; it creates in us a capacity for
the closest possible intimacy with God.

—Monica Baldwin

Pastor Chris, what do you think about the latest Supreme
Court ruling?"

"Pastor, what's your opinion on how to treat the LGBT community?"

"Chris, what's your view on this terrible tragedy that just
happened?"

Every day it seems various people—from members of our
church and fellow Christians to reporters and bloggers—ask me
what I think about that day's headlines. Whether it's about the
definition of marriage, a new state law, or the latest shooting, my
answer is the same.

"What makes you think *my* opinion matters?" I say. "What
difference does it make what you or I think about this? The only
opinion that matters is God's."

Of course, we live in a culture that's social-media obsessed with
personal opinions, comments, likes, and retweets. We've become
the center of our own little universes, and virtually everything
around us reinforces the delusion that we can and should control

our own destinies—and offer our two cents on how everyone else is controlling theirs. We seem to think everyone's opinion matters but that whoever can defend theirs the best or shout the loudest wins. But this obsession is really only another major symptom of the cultural cancer plaguing our society—the sin of pride.

It doesn't matter what our friends on Facebook, our employers' HR departments, or our favorite celebrities think about anything. If we're committed to knowing, loving, and serving God, then it doesn't matter what we think. We have to focus on what God thinks. And he's given us his Word to guide us in knowing what he thinks. If God has already spoken, then we don't need to form an opinion. We just need to keep pursuing the way, the truth, and the life that can be found only in Jesus.

This dedicated pursuit requires us to humble ourselves before the Lord and to realize that he knows best—we don't. It's not easy, but it's one of the most important parts of standing strong when the winds of culture start to blow. It's one of the most urgent warnings we must heed from the example of Daniel.

Full of Pride

So far we've focused on culture's greatest goal (trying to change our identity) and culture's greatest test (pulling us away from worshipping God). Now it's time to consider our culture's greatest sin: pride. *Pride* is

> To stay healthy, we must stay humble.

one of those words that has come to be synonymous with self-confidence and strength of character. And while there's nothing wrong with a healthy sense of self, I believe to stay healthy, we must stay humble. Anytime we feel like we're better than another person, or another group of people, then pride inflates our egos. Anytime we place ourselves before God, we're in even bigger trouble.

Pride is a "gateway" sin that offers an open doorway for our Enemy to drop in and tell us just how great we are and how we really don't need God. It whispers, "Religion is just a crutch for all those weak people! You're strong; you're better than that. You're in control of your life." These lies embolden us to question God and to start thinking he doesn't know what he's doing, to start believing we know more than God knows.

But you and I know that's not true. God's Word could not be clearer about the magnificence, power, and holiness of God—or about the sinfulness, weaknesses, and limitations of humanity. Pride is a massive problem that usually creates a chain reaction of massive consequences. This is why the issue of pride appears again and again in the prophetic books of the Bible. It leads to so many other sinful choices and actions.

Prophetic warnings in Scripture are there to get us to turn away from our sin and to return to God. They are also there to point out the consequences if we don't make a U-turn in our hearts and repent. The book of Daniel places such a warning front and center throughout the entire story, asking us to consider how to live a godly life in an ungodly age.

> Pride is a massive problem that usually creates a chain reaction of massive consequences.

Daniel wrote not only to share his experiences and God's faithfulness in Babylon but also to inform, encourage, and warn other believers in the end times. Covering almost seventy-five years of Daniel's life, this book bearing his name is more relevant to us today than ever before. As we watch our culture disintegrate into moral chaos and heart-wrenching violence, Daniel's warning to us echoes throughout our daily headlines.

And it's only growing louder.

Dangerous Thoughts

The issue of human pride, arrogance, and self-sufficiency has never loomed larger than it does today. People think they can custom design the DNA of their babies, change their gender, or scientifically prevent death. We're told if we can attain enough money, then we can control virtually every detail in our lives. The need for God is slowly being replaced by reliance on science, devotion to the Internet, and the pursuit of personal happiness. It's devastating to witness this widespread deception by the Enemy creep into our neighborhoods, churches, and families.

In the book of Daniel, we see these same attitudes in King Nebuchadnezzar. Maybe you've heard of the Hanging Gardens of Babylon, one of the Seven Wonders of the ancient world. They were an architectural and horticultural masterpiece, an accomplishment that merged artistic talent with the technology of the day. They were built under the reign of Nebuchadnezzar. With this great feat, coupled with his leadership in conquering the Israelites, he probably felt like he was the greatest king the Babylonians had ever known—maybe he even considered himself the greatest monarch in the world.

Interestingly, the issue of Nebuchadnezzar's pride did not emerge until after he had committed to accepting the Most High God, the God of Daniel and his people. After witnessing not one but several miracles with Daniel and his Hebrew friends, the king could not deny the power and divinity of this God. In fact, the king made a joyful proclamation:

> King Nebuchadnezzar,
>
> To the nations and peoples of every language, who live in all the earth:
>
> May you *prosper* greatly! It is my pleasure to tell you about

the miraculous signs and wonders that the Most High God has performed for me.

> How great are his signs,
>   how mighty his wonders!
> His kingdom is an eternal kingdom;
>   his dominion endures from generation to generation.
>   (Dan. 4:1–3, emphasis mine)

The word used for "prosper" here is the same Hebrew word that is used for "peace." And it encompasses more than just a restful, quiet state of being. This kind of prosperity means peace in our souls, a sense of well-being and fulfillment that nothing can disturb, even if everything around you crumbles into chaos.

But for Nebuchadnezzar peace did not come easy.

His pride got in the way.

Just like it does for us.

As You Like It

Have you ever thought about how destructive pride is in our lives? It's the root of every other sin. The worst sin isn't murder or adultery; it's pride. Pride declares, "I want to be God! I will choose my own way and live as I please." But, as Nebuchadnezzar's story reveals, this kind of pride only leads to insanity, the disease of deranged thinking, the inner turmoil of discontent. His story reveals that we can choose either humility or humiliation. One you can initiate, and the other God will initiate.

In fact, God warned Nebuchadnezzar about this and identified three areas where pride often flourishes, choking out humility and a healthy fear of the Lord. The first is prosperity and contentment, a sense of complacency that becomes our entitlement to enjoy all that life has to offer, whatever we want. We're told, "I, Nebuchadnezzar, was at home in my palace, contented and prosperous" (Dan. 4:4).

When times are good, we may not think about God much. If our bills are paid, our family is healthy, and we have enough to eat and a roof over our heads, we might not think we need God. Everything is going well enough without him, right? So why worship God and acknowledge him as the source when we don't have to? Most of us don't know how to handle prosperity.

But when times are hard, where do we turn? When our circumstances are beyond our control, when our children are sick in a way that baffles doctors, when our retirement savings disappears overnight, when we're shocked by the divorce papers, that's when we turn to God for help. We know we can't change certain circumstances, and we need supernatural power and intervention to survive them.

If we want to overcome pride in our lives, then we must turn from being self-sufficient back to being God-dependent. We must give him the credit for everything we have and acknowledge that we're just stewards of these many blessings. God doesn't bless us just so we can hoard a lot of money and buy stuff. He blesses us to be a blessing for others, to advance his kingdom, to reveal his love through the gift of salvation in Christ.

How do we express our dependence on God? Like so many aspects of our relationship with the Lord, it begins with prayer. God's Word says, "If [God's] people . . . humble themselves and pray" then he will hear us and forgive us (2 Chron. 7:14). The act of simply coming before God in prayer indicates a willingness to surrender ourselves to him. Have you ever thought about the "atheism of prayerlessness" and contrasted it with the way we all cry out to God in a crisis?[1] True dependence on God relies on prayer as a consistent lifeline—every day and not just when the going gets tough.

I know firsthand that I can do nothing without remaining in constant contact with my Father. So many people ask me to tell them the secret to our health and growth at Church of the Highlands. Several times a year I'll go to conferences and speak to thousands of pastors, and they all ask the same thing: "How did you get all those people at your church?" I'm used to seeing a look of disappointment on their faces, because I always give the same answer: "Prayer. We stay dependent on God." There's nothing flashy or unusual or special. We just pray.

> True dependence on God relies on prayer as a consistent lifeline—every day and not just when the going gets tough.

I know that's the answer to why our church has grown and flourished, because I know very clearly who I am. To be honest, I'm simply not smart enough or talented enough to try and take any of the credit. I was a C student in school—and I worked hard for most of those "average" grades. I used to get so ticked at all the over-achieving A students who always had to mess up the grading curve.

The only reason I have had such a strong relationship with the Lord today is because I know who I am on my own and I stay dependent on God for everything in my life. The more our ministries have grown, the more campuses we have, the more members who join us here, as well as in other cities, the more I have prayed and the more I have asked, urged, and requested others to pray for me and our leaders and everyone in our church family and communities.

In fact, you may remember me sharing about the 21 Days of Prayer (21days.churchofthehighlands.com) earlier, during which we commit the beginning of every year to coming together as a church and fasting and praying for three weeks. We listen for

God's voice and seek his guidance. We worship and honor him as the Lord of our lives and the loving Father of our hearts. We do it every January because we want to show God that he comes first, that before we do anything else in a new year, we want to seek him and grow closer. We are dependent on him and him alone.

Whenever I'm scheduled to speak or preach, I always hold a prayer meeting the day before. Back when I was in youth ministry and teaching kids on Wednesday nights, I'd invite about a hundred out of the thousand to come over to my house and pray with me and for me. They always raided my fridge and cleared the pantry, but it was a small price to pay.

Even now—especially now—I meet on Saturdays at the church with a group of dedicated prayer warriors. We pray together, read prayer requests from members, and walk around and pray over the seats where thousands of people will be sitting the next day. Not only does it keep me dependent on God, but it also reminds me to stay humble, to put my ego and my pride aside. Not my will but his.

If there's any secret, it's simply to stay dependent on God—all the time.

Where Credit Is Due

The second area where pride undermines our spiritual growth is in our attitude toward getting or giving credit. Do we take credit for what we have and enjoy in our lives, or do we give thanks to God and acknowledge his goodness as the source? King Nebuchadnezzar discovered his answer through a powerfully disturbing dream, which Daniel interpreted.

In his dream, the king saw a magnificent tree whose lush branches provided fruit, shade, and cover for many people and animals. But then a heavenly messenger called out for the tree to be cut down and its various parts dispersed (Dan. 4:5–21). The king's advisors and magicians could not interpret the dream, so Daniel was brought in. And while Nebuchadnezzar hoped that the tree represented his enemies whom he had leveled, Daniel made it clear this was not the case:

> Your Majesty, you are that tree! You have become great and strong; your greatness has grown until it reaches the sky, and your dominion extends to distant parts of the earth.
>
> Your Majesty saw a holy one, a messenger, coming down from heaven and saying, "Cut down the tree and destroy it, but leave the stump, bound with iron and bronze, in the grass of the field, while its roots remain in the ground. Let him be drenched with the dew of heaven; let him live with the wild animals, until seven times pass by for him."
>
> This is the interpretation, Your Majesty, and this is the decree the Most High has issued against my lord the king: You will be driven away from people and will live with the wild animals; you will eat grass like the ox and be drenched with the dew of heaven. Seven times will pass by for you until you acknowledge that the Most High is sovereign over all kingdoms on earth and gives them to anyone he wishes. (Dan. 4:22–25)

Nebuchadnezzar was clearly a legend in his own mind! He praised himself quite a bit—after all, he was the king who built the Hanging Gardens and conquered Israel. But he failed to realize that everything came from God. It was God who equipped him to be king and allowed him to oversee the achievements he so proudly claimed as his own. Every breath, every meal, every relationship, every possession—it all came from God.

Notice the warning, though. It pointed out the natural consequences of such arrogance and pride. It was not a threat of how

God would punish him; it was simply highlighting the result of thinking he was better than God. And it's a warning we would all be wise to heed. If we allow our self-pride to grow, it will lead to insanity. People tend to think God brings judgment, *but we bring it upon ourselves.*

So what can we do to avoid the same fate as Nebuchadnezzar? What's the best way to pull the weeds of pride in our life's garden? Having an attitude of gratitude. Worshipping and giving God thanks and praise yanks out those stubborn thoughts and words of the Enemy, especially the ones that try to give us the credit and not God. When we declare that everything comes from God, it restores our perspective. It straightens out our thinking and reminds us of what's true. It revives our sanity.

I know it can be challenging to be grateful when you're suffering through tough circumstances, but I'm reminded of a prayer request I read recently during one of our Saturday prayer meetings. It was from a dear older woman in our church, Miss Anita. She requested prayer for healing from a surgery in which her leg was amputated. Faced with the pain and debilitation of this life-changing condition, Miss Anita also wrote, "Thank you so much for your prayers! I feel so blessed to be here at this church. God is so good to me, and I'm just so grateful for all his many blessings."

I had to reread her request a couple of times to make sure I understood it correctly. Here was this dear lady with an amputated leg thanking me for praying for her and telling me how good God has been to her. Yes, just so you know, there may have been a slight mist coming from my eyes. That kind of faith and gratitude is a testimony. It's the exact opposite of Nebuchadnezzar's gardens and monuments, his military victories and palaces.

Success and prosperity can blind us. We erroneously think we earned it and it's ours. But the truth is that it's all God's. The Bible asks us, "What are you so puffed up about? What do you have that God hasn't given you? And if all you have is from God, why act as though you have accomplished something on your own?" (1 Cor. 4:7 TLB). I remember this every time I give a tithe or an offering by praying a simple prayer: *Lord, this is yours—all of it is yours. Thank you.*

Heaven Rules

Finally, the third area where we must uproot pride in our lives is in our perspective. We must stop thinking that we know best and acknowledge that heaven rules. We see this play out in the last part of the king's dream. Daniel explained, "The command to leave the stump of the tree with its roots means that your kingdom will be restored to you when you acknowledge that Heaven rules" (Dan. 4:26).

God always shows us the way back; he's always willing to produce new growth from the stumps in our lives. When our pride causes us to fall under the weight of our own arrogance, then we're forced to humble ourselves and start over. God will meet us there if we're willing to humble ourselves and ask him. If we're willing to acknowledge that heaven rules, not us here on earth. This is how we regain God's favor in our lives.

> This is the essence of sin in a nutshell: my way instead of God's way.

But Nebuchadnezzar learned this the hard way. He went through seven years of living like a madman, a wild animal, out of his mind. He wasn't allowed to be around his own people. He ate grass and quit acting human (Dan. 4:33). Basically, he lost not only his clarity and peace of mind but his very humanity.

The same is true for us today. When we do not heed God's warning, our pride causes us to collapse under the weight of our sins. We are living in a generation in which everyone is wise in their own eyes. There's a complete disregard for the standards set by God's Word. Think about it: Did you ever imagine yourself living in a culture where phrases like "recreational drug use," "sex buddy," and "gay marriage" would exist, let alone be heard every day?

Some people like to call our age "progressive" and imply that God and his ways are outdated and archaic. But this is the essence of sin in a nutshell: my way instead of God's way.

Whose rules do you live by?

Your own? Or heaven's?

Sanity Restored

Nebuchadnezzar chose to live by his own rules, ignored God's warning, and paid the price. The prophecy was fulfilled. We also have ignored God's many warnings, and now we see the prophecy fulfilled all around us. Where do we go from here?

Fortunately, Nebuchadnezzar eventually came to his senses and returned to God in full humility. He finally heeded Daniel's advice, wisdom that still holds true as the remedy for our own individual and cultural pride: "Therefore, Your Majesty, be pleased to accept my advice: Renounce your sins by doing what is right, and your wickedness by being kind to the oppressed. It may be that then your prosperity will continue" (Dan. 4:27). After his seven years of madness, here's what Nebuchadnezzar said—which is also what we need to say:

> At the end of that time, I, Nebuchadnezzar, raised my eyes toward heaven, and my sanity was restored. Then I praised the Most High; I honored and glorified him who lives forever.
>
> His dominion is an eternal dominion;
> his kingdom endures from generation to generation.

All the peoples of the earth
    are regarded as nothing.
He does as he pleases
    with the powers of heaven
    and the peoples of the earth.
No one can hold back his hand
    or say to him: "What have you done?"

At the same time that my sanity was restored, my honor and splendor were returned to me for the glory of my kingdom. My advisers and nobles sought me out, and I was restored to my throne and became even greater than before. Now I, Nebuchadnezzar, praise and exalt and glorify the King of heaven, because everything he does is right and all his ways are just. And those who walk in pride he is able to humble. (Dan. 4:34–37)

What a great prayer to pray! God responded immediately to the king's humble prayer and restored him to a clear mind, a peaceful heart, and a joyful life. God is always ready to respond to a broken heart. He is our loving Father and is always willing to forgive.

Do you want your sanity restored in the midst of a crazy culture? Would you like to have peace in your soul as the turmoil of godless tragedies unfold around you? With the repentant king of Babylon as our example, let's focus on three steps.

First, exalt the King of heaven. God deserves heartfelt praise; anything less is arrogance on our part. Previously I mentioned my frustration with the way people will go wild at football games and other sporting events but roll their eyes at the thought of raising their hands during a worship song. And sports isn't the only cultural arena where people engage in passionate worship. Just consider how many thousands of concert-goers remain on their feet, clapping, waving, and singing along with their favorite pop star, rock icon, or touring band.

I have a dream that one day the praise at Church of the Highlands on Sunday will be greater than the praise that happens in football stadiums and concert venues. God has asked us to praise him and even told us how to do it. We owe it to him to give him all the praise we can! Not just in church, but every day. We should be people who are grateful in all circumstances—people others stop and notice because of the way we continue to express thankfulness to God.

Next, acknowledge that God does everything right and all his ways are just. More than ever, accept the authority of God's Word. Don't second-guess him. Don't try to figure everything out. Don't try to change the Bible to fit what you want it to say. God's ways are higher—simply accept that as you obey them!

Remember, God doesn't ask us to try to understand his ways. He knows we simply can't, so he doesn't expect us to try. He just asks us to obey him. To trust him. It's actually very liberating to trust in something you do not have to understand.

We won't always agree with what he asks us to do, but if we love him, then we still obey him. This is how we let him be God and surrender ourselves to him. The day you do, your sanity will be restored and peace will flood your soul. I'm convinced the day our country returns to its Judeo-Christian values is the day sanity will be restored to our country.

> Humility is not thinking less of yourself; *humility is thinking of yourself less.*

Finally, walk in humility. This doesn't mean putting yourself down all the time or being a doormat. "Oh, don't mind me—I'm just a lowly little speck in the universe." Some people think this is spiritual, but it's not. Humility is not thinking less of yourself; *humility is thinking of yourself less.*

We can be courageous and contrite at the same time. Walking in humility is an attitude. We're told, "Humble yourselves before the Lord, and he will lift you up" (James 4:10). We actually grow closer to God when we're less focused on ourselves.

We will all certainly be humbled in this life. We can choose to humble ourselves before God, or he will humble us by allowing us to face the consequences of our sin. Nebuchadnezzar reminds us that it's a whole lot better if we humble ourselves instead of resisting God.

Another powerful example of humility before God is my pastor growing up, Brother Roy Stockstill. I'm so grateful for the amazing Christian heritage I had, both in my family and within my church family. Bethany Church in Baton Rouge, Louisiana, was my home church during some of the most formative years of my life.

> Standing strong in a pride-inflated culture begins facedown.

Brother Roy founded Bethany in 1962, and under his leadership it became one of the most influential churches in the world. But he remained one of the meekest, gentlest, most humble men I've ever met.

He recently went to be with the Lord, and I was honored for the opportunity to eulogize him at his memorial service. Brother Roy was known for his "sayings," and I enjoyed sharing some of my favorites over the years. When teaching on humility, Brother Roy would say, "If you start your day on your face before the Lord, there's nowhere to go but up. The man on his face can never fall from that position."

Standing strong in a pride-inflated culture begins facedown.

Humble yourself before the Lord.

And he will meet you there.

Eight

THE ART OF DYING

Control your emotions or they will control you.

—CHINESE PROVERB

D ad, I'm sooo tired. Can I stay home today?" my daughter said with sleepy eyes, barely raising her head from her pillow.

"Of course, honey—good idea," I said before quietly closing her door and moving on to my son's room. Being the good dad I am, I wanted her to get as much rest as she needed and to just get up whenever she thought it time.

"Hey, buddy, it's time to wake up. Bus will be here in forty-five minutes."

No response but a light snore followed by, "Sleepy . . . Can I go in late, please?"

"Well . . ."

"Please, Dad?"

"Okay, sure thing, son," I said. "Sleep is much more important than your English test. You can go whenever you wake up and feel like going."

At that exact moment, my alarm went off and, boy, was I grateful to wake up from this nightmare. Let my kids sleep late just because they felt like it? I don't think so! Raising five kids, Tammy and I discovered the great paradox of sleep: when they're little, you can't get them to sleep, and when they're older, you can't get them to wake up! Getting everyone to bed on time and up on time used to feel like working the air-traffic control tower at O'Hare.

As frustrating as it was at times, both for them and for us, we knew we had to make this choice. While the kids thought we were trying to torture them, we loved them and simply wanted what was best for them in the long run. Parents can see the value that today's choices have on tomorrow's success. If we let our kids live according to what they felt like doing, then they would never sleep well, eat healthy food, or go to school. Most of the time, doing what's best for our children directly contrasts with what they feel.

The Folly of Feelings

Kids aren't the only ones who prefer to live by their feelings as opposed to what's best for them. The same is true for many adults. Consider the way many of us act when we're dealing with relationships. When we're infatuated or, heaven forbid, "in love," we become blind to logic and reality and only want to do what's best

> God is more interested in your character than your comfort.

"for the relationship." Many bad decisions are made when feelings are in control. And then our feelings fade. Whether it's feeling in love or road-rage angry, those emotions eventually pass like a storm front.

In fact, the compulsion to lead with our feelings is probably one of the greatest challenges to living by faith. Many times I've sat across from another man in our church who is trying to justify leaving his wife so he can be with his new "soul mate." His rationale is that God wants him to be happy, right? So isn't it better to be with the person he "truly loves" rather than the woman he married all those years ago when he was "in a different place"? My response is never what these guys want to hear, but it's always the same: God is more interested in your character than your comfort. He would rather have you holy than happy.

It's not that feelings are bad or dangerous in and of themselves. God made us to be emotional creatures who feel deeply. No, the problem with feelings is one of emphasis, of order, of priorities. Simply put, our choices must lead and our feelings will follow. If we only make decisions based on how we feel in the moment, then our decisions will lead us into all kinds of trouble. We simply can't rely on our feelings to guide us.

You may have heard this comparison before, but it's a good one. Our feelings are like fire. When contained and focused properly, fire gives us warmth, cooks our food, and refines metal. But when left unchecked, a spark can become a wildfire in a matter of seconds, burning millions of acres. The same fire that provides so many benefits when contained by a brick fireplace can reduce everything in its path to ash when given free rein.

> Our choices must lead and our feelings will follow.

Similarly, our feelings have wonderful potential to help us experience the joy, peace, and fullness of being alive. The psalmist wrote, "Take delight in the LORD, and he will give you the desires of your heart" (Ps. 37:4). Notice that it's only after we take delight in the Lord that he gives us the desires of our hearts. Because when we are focused on God and delighting in our relationship with him, the desires of our hearts naturally revolve around what he wants for our lives. In other words, because we've made a choice to place God first in our lives, our emotions follow our will.

Remember, feelings are a gift from God—they're not the problem. The problem is when we allow our feelings to make choices and motivate our actions. If we want to stand strong in a bow-down culture, we must first choose whom we will serve and then contain the fiery power of our emotions so they can be used in constructive ways to love God and serve others.

If It Feels Good . . .

Even when we place God first in our lives, it doesn't mean we won't be tempted to let our feelings occasionally lead us. All throughout Scripture, we see numerous stories about people who followed their feelings, especially when they weren't following God. In fact, the people of Israel did just that, as recorded in the book of Judges: "At that time there was no king in Israel. People did whatever they felt like doing" (21:25 MSG). Just as we experience today, following their emotions led to the Israelites' downfall. Letting our feelings lead the way always produces chaos.

In contrast, one of the consistent aspects we see in Daniel's character is the way he governed himself based on choices and commitments, not feelings and fantasies. Daniel knew his motivation for saying no, which enabled him to give the king the same answer in various circumstances—from the time he was beckoned to eat the monarch's unhealthy diet to the time he had to watch his three friends face the fiery furnace rather than denounce their faith in God. When it became even more personal and Daniel himself was thrown into the lions' den, his natural feelings of fear, anxiety, and perhaps even anger were probably multiplied.

But regardless of what Daniel may have felt, his faith—like his convictions—remained solid through and through. They were not based on his mood, comfort, or ability to understand or agree with what God was doing. Despite the full range of human emotions Daniel may have experienced throughout his seventy years in captivity, he chose to exercise his own free will in refusing to back down when faced with the cultural pressure of the Babylonians. His decisions were not based on circumstances, excuses, or rationalizations. They were based on his trust in God.

We have the same ability to choose. God doesn't want us to be his puppets; he loves us enough to let us choose between saying yes to him and no to our flesh or saying no to him and yes to our own desires. When he gave us that free will, it opened the door for us to make selfish, feelings-based choices, away from him. This is the very issue that caused Adam and Eve to sin, and it's the same problem prevalent in our culture today.

So many people believe that Christianity is no longer relevant to our culture or our needs, both individually and corporately. Relying on God's Word as the basis for making choices is seen as an outdated way of thinking and living. But that's simply not the case. In fact, the Bible predicts this very philosophy. We see this clearly in the New Testament's collection of letters written to the Corinthian church. In many ways, the city of Corinth had a lot in common with our American culture today. It was quite wealthy, humanistic, and arrogant. It placed human intellect above spiritual law and hedonistic pleasure above self-discipline and obedience to God. "If it feels good, do it!" could easily have been a bumper sticker on chariots in Corinth.

Paul hit the Corinthian culture head-on by challenging its reliance on the "wisdom of the world." He pointed out the difference between someone who lives only for themself and someone who lives for Christ:

> For the message of the cross is foolishness to those who are perishing, but to us who are being saved it is the power of God. For it is written:
> "I will destroy the wisdom of the wise;
>   the intelligence of the intelligent I will frustrate."

Where is the wise person? Where is the teacher of the law? Where is the philosopher of this age? Has not God made foolish the wisdom of the world? (1 Cor. 1:18–20)

Notice the progression of Paul's thinking here. The world thinks Christianity is archaic, but we know differently because we've experienced the power of God to change our lives (v. 18). God frustrates and destroys the world's wisdom, which only frustrates worldly people even more (v. 19). This is important because it establishes that we don't have to argue our beliefs. In the end, God's way works and all other ways don't. God's truth is self-evident. It's not up to us to convince nonbelievers that God's way is the right way. But we *can* lovingly engage in conversations in which we seek to understand where they're coming from and what they've been through. We *can* be a constant source of encouragement in the life of someone who doesn't know God.

Finally, Paul concluded that God's ways, which are higher than anyone's ability to comprehend, make the wisdom of the world look foolish (v. 20). Paul explained, "For the foolishness of God is wiser than human wisdom, and the weakness of God is stronger than human strength" (v. 25). This must be our theme as we engage with the culture and its worldly wisdom. As believers, we must affirm this principal truth regularly. Because all of hell wants us to replace God's truth with the "new norm."

Feelings vs. Faith

So how did we get to this place where our feelings are more accepted than God's wisdom? For that matter, how does any generation arrive at this brink of desperation? I'm a firm believer that you can't fix something you can't see, so let's consider the main components that have led us to our world today. These are the same two ingredients present anytime we allow ourselves to be consumed by the culture around us.

First, we followed our feelings instead of our faith.

Despite what God's Word says, and in spite of our own past experiences, we still tend to think our feelings can be trusted. We think reality consists of whatever we feel. Regardless of what our feelings may be, we assume that they reflect how God made us, therefore earning his stamp of approval. As I said before, it's good to have feelings—they help us engage with God, other people, and the world around us in extraordinary ways. But it's not okay to call our feelings our truth. God is the only One who has cornered the market on truth. Our emotions, opinions, and desires don't determine truth. It's not a subjective commodity to be determined by each individual. God's eternal truth exists regardless of what we feel or don't feel.

In many cases, our feelings leave us vulnerable to temptations. The apostle Paul warned us about letting our feelings take over: "So letting your sinful nature control your mind leads to death. But letting the Spirit control your mind leads to life and peace" (Rom. 8:6 NLT). Keep in mind that being tempted is not wrong. After all, Jesus was tempted, but he never gave in and committed a sin. So we shouldn't shame or condemn anyone—including ourselves—simply for having feelings or for feeling a certain way. As long as we seek God more than anything or anyone else, then we should embrace feelings in a healthy way and use them to further our purpose and enjoyment of life. As long as we're willing to

> As long as we're willing to repent of our sins and accept God's grace and forgiveness, we can focus our feelings to follow our faith.

repent of our sins and accept God's grace and forgiveness, we can focus our feelings to follow our faith.

The real test comes when we have to decide how we will define sin in our lives and the lives of others. Will we agree with God's definition of sin based on his Word? Or will we, instead, trust our feelings to be our guide?

Second, we trusted ourselves more than we trusted God.

Here's the real reason we ended up culturally bankrupt: we think we know best. We think we know best about marriage, sex, parenting, money—about everything. But who are we to define something we didn't create? Doesn't it make more sense that the One who created it would know more? Are we going to trust culture's new norm, or are we going to trust God?

It's time to make a break. It's time to refuse to follow the norm. It's time to refuse to abandon our faith. The world may think we're old-fashioned, but we know that God's truth is the source for true liberation and authentic freedom. His principles don't constrict and inhibit us; they give us full, abundant life. They give us peace, joy, purpose, and fulfillment.

The world promises that if we follow our own bliss, we'll find happiness. But I have yet to see anyone who attests to this. In fact, the evidence continues to point in the opposite direction. Recent research comparing teens who lack a solid, biblical belief system with their peers who have one reveals that teens who lack a solid, biblical belief system are:

- 225% more likely to be angry with life
- 216% more likely to be resentful
- 210% more likely to lack purpose in life
- 200% more likely to be disappointed in life

- 200% more likely to steal
- 200% more likely to physically hurt someone
- 300% more likely to use illegal drugs
- 600% more likely to attempt suicide[1]

If these statistics break your heart, I'm with you. I can't help but think about the teens in our neighborhoods, classrooms, and communities whom these numbers represent. What a reminder that we have to choose first and let our feelings follow. Without having a basis for our beliefs that's grounded in ultimate truth, we will succumb to the roller-coaster ride of living by our emotions. One day we'll be up, then the next we'll be disappointed and angry, and on another we'll be afraid. Our moods often swing 180 degrees based on a variety of factors—circumstances, physical health, diet, and relationships with other people. God's truth, however, remains the same yesterday, today, and forever.

You Can't Always Get What You Want

So what's the secret to not being a "feelings-based" Christian? The Bible couldn't be clearer: we must learn to crucify our flesh and live like Jesus. Paul explained, "I have been crucified with Christ and I no longer live, but Christ lives in me. The life I now live in the body, I live by faith in the Son of God, who loved me and gave himself for me" (Gal. 2:20).

I realize this probably isn't the solution you wanted to hear. Whenever I preach on this passage, I know it's not a message that's going to attract new members and grow the church. Instead, it's a message that's going to grow people into being more like Jesus Christ. This is where the rubber meets the road and we put what we believe to the test of daily life.

Jesus faced this dilemma long before he was arrested and hung on a cross to die. He taught this principle of sacrificing our selfish desires to accomplish what his Father calls us to do. Nearing the end of his earthly ministry, Christ had a heated exchange with one of his disciples over this very issue:

> From that time on Jesus began to explain to his disciples that he must go to Jerusalem and suffer many things at the hands of the elders, the chief priests and the teachers of the law, and that he must be killed and on the third day be raised to life.
>
> Peter took him aside and began to rebuke him. "Never, Lord!" he said. "This shall never happen to you!"
>
> Jesus turned and said to Peter, "Get behind me, Satan! You are a stumbling block to me; you do not have in mind the concerns of God, but merely human concerns."
>
> Then Jesus said to his disciples, "Whoever wants to be my disciple must deny themselves and take up their cross and follow me. For whoever wants to save their life will lose it, but whoever loses their life for me will find it." (Matt. 16:21–25)

Notice Peter's frustration and anger in this situation. Like many of Jesus' disciples, he assumed Christ had been sent to establish an earthly kingdom. But God's plan was much bigger than this. He wasn't establishing a social, political, or military kingdom; he was establishing an eternal, heavenly, forgiven kingdom. But Peter wasn't getting this at the time. He was simply upset that his agenda wasn't happening.

Instead of becoming the new king of Israel, Jesus told his disciples, he would be falsely arrested, sentenced to death, and executed like a common criminal. This must have boggled Peter's mind! You can always tell if you've gone back to your old way of life by your level of frustration when you don't get what you want. But notice how the Master responded to Peter's abrupt outburst. I suspect he wasn't even addressing Peter; instead, Jesus spoke directly to the Enemy at work within the situation. Basically, he said, "You're not focusing on God's perspective and plan here; you're focused on a limited, human view." This is the root issue of the problem with putting our feelings first: they lie. They are not accurate about the things that matter most.

Then Jesus gave the solution, and it's a painful remedy: deny yourself and give up what feels like life to you and take up your cross. To follow Jesus and have new life—eternal life—something has to die. Following him and not the way of the world often hurts. I like to think of this friction as spiritual growing pains.

It's a hard message to hear, and it sounds counterintuitive. To find life, we have to lose it. The great irony, of course, is that if we follow Christ and put to death our old way of life, then we discover the freedom and joy that only comes from knowing and loving him. This is the source of true life! Paul, writing to the Romans, described it this way: "For we know that our old self was crucified with him so that the body ruled by sin might be done away with, that we should no longer be slaves to sin—because anyone who has died has been set free from sin" (Rom. 6:6–7).

> We want God to change our circumstances. But God wants to change *us*.

Too often we want God to change our circumstances. But God wants to change *us*. He wants us to grow and mature and develop fully into the men and women he created us to be. When self dies, we are set free. Our Father loves us so much and wants us to choose to give up what can't make us happy—even though we may feel like it can—to gain true eternal joy. If you let him change you, you will be the happiest person you know!

Living the Crucified Life

The "crucified life" is not something many of us understand—or want to understand. How, exactly, do we live this "crucified life"? What does it look like? How do we live out this paradox that to live we have to die?

Once again, we find wisdom in Paul's letter to the Galatians. There he mentions crucifixion three separate times.

Too Much You, Not Enough Him

The first instance of crucifixion occurs in the verse we read earlier in this chapter: "I have been crucified with Christ and I no longer live" (Gal. 2:20). This makes it clear *we must crucify self.* This process begins during our salvation experience, which many people often consider a one-time event—you know, that time you walked down to the front of the church and prayed for Jesus to forgive your sins and enter your heart.

But Paul indicates that our salvation involves ongoing crucifixion of our fleshly desires: "I face death every day" (1 Cor. 15:31). Paul learned the discipline of dying daily to keep from going back to his former habits and ways of life. Again, what does this look like, practically speaking?

> Every day I want to see how low I can go. Less of me. More of him.

While dying to self varies in particular actions, I believe it begins with an attitude of daily humility. Every morning when I wake up, I thank God and give him my life again for the rest of that day. Every part of my body, my time, my energy, my resources—everything I have, I give to him yet again. I like to kneel during this prayer time of full submission to my Lord each day because it reminds me, "He must become *greater and greater*, and I must become *less and less*" (John 3:30 NLT, emphasis mine). Every day I want to see how low I can go. Less of me. More of him.

If you're not enjoying your life, if it doesn't feel like you're experiencing the full, abundant life Jesus said he came to bring us, then the problem likely starts in one place. There's too much you and not enough him.

Battle of the Beach

Paul's second reference to crucifixion in Galatians says, "Those who belong to Christ Jesus have crucified the flesh with its passions and desires" (5:24). This is basically *crucifying our sinful nature*, those natural feelings and desires and longings apart from God. This kind of death may be the most painful, because our flesh is directly tied in to our feelings.

We all have passions and desires that don't line up with God's Word. Too often we make excuses for them and justify the actions and behaviors they precipitate. "Sorry, that's just who I am. That's the way God made me. Just my particular predisposition and orientation. Nothing I can do to change it."

No, this is our flesh talking! We can't make excuses for our sinful appetites and natural weaknesses or accept them simply as part of who we are, as if there's nothing to be done but give in to them. We don't have to listen to our passions. We can crucify them and find real freedom.

Listen: if I followed my feelings and listened to my flesh, I wouldn't be a pastor right now. I have feelings and physical desires every day that are in conflict with God's Word. Just as many men experience, one of my greatest battles involves feelings of attraction to women who are not my wife.

For this reason, I absolutely hate going to the beach. I hate everything about it—the sun, the sand, the heat, the sunburn, the sunscreen, the water, the jellyfish. And, most of all, I hate going to the beach because I know I'll have to do battle. It's a given that on almost any beach there will be women exposing most of their bodies. Many of these will be beautiful, attractive, and alluring. So I will inevitably have to engage in a battle against my flesh, which would love to flirt, chat, and do a whole lot more with these women.

But I've already made choices. To honor God and obey his Word. To love my wife and to honor the vows of marriage to which I committed. To respect my position as a shepherd of God's people and to maintain my integrity as a leader who inherently sets an example for others. These choices were made long ago. My line in the sand, as I shared with you earlier, has been drawn.

Because I have made these choices, when my feelings threaten mutiny, I don't accept them. Instead, I crucify them. My feelings don't define me. My choices do.

Can you see, then, why our pleasure-first culture is so troubling? It's like slow-motion, spiritual suicide. So many people justify their actions because of their feelings. "I have to live my own truth," people often say to me, "because that's just how I feel." I see the self-destructive path they're on and want to warn them and yell (but usually try to talk at normal volume), *"Nooo—you don't! You don't have to believe what the world is telling you. There is something better. Your feelings don't define truth—only God does!"*

> We know what our flesh wants. And we must decide to put it to death every day.

Many people today say, "Let me love however I feel like loving." They justify practices in direct conflict with Scripture because it's what their physical bodies desire and want to do. I don't deny those desires are real; I just know that feelings cannot be trusted to define truth.

When those engaging in premarital sex, practicing homosexuality, or indulging in any other sexual sin justify their actions on the basis of their natural feelings, I always want to ask why they think they should get a free pass. In other words, God calls us to consciously put away our natural inclinations toward sin, so why would anyone be exempt from this and be allowed or even encouraged to act on their sexual feelings regardless of what God has said in his Word?

Every morning when we wake up, we must make choices. We know what our flesh wants. And we must decide to put it to death every day. The Bible says, "*Choose* for yourselves this day whom you will serve. . . . But as for me and my household, we will serve the LORD" (Josh. 24:15, emphasis mine).

Who are you serving today?
Who do you want to serve?
What needs to die for you to have life?
What fleshly desires must you crucify?

Choices and Changes

Paul answered these questions with his third and final reference to crucifixion in Galatians: "May I never boast except in the cross of our Lord Jesus Christ, through which the world has been crucified to me, and I to the world" (6:14). Paul's secret was to *use the cross of Christ as a filter for viewing the world.* Jesus was Paul's standard and reference point, his true north on life's compass, the basis for evaluating everything he encountered.

Paul is well known for his travels throughout the ancient world, where he encountered a variety of cultures and religious practices. He likely faced temptation in a variety of forms, from sensual and lustful pursuits like the ones he found in Rome to temptations to abandon his calling and settle down in one safe, comfortable locale. But filtering these opportunities through the cross of Christ, Paul realized that they would be sinful, fulfilling his own desires and not God's standards. These temptations would lead him away from God instead of closer to Christ.

We've all got to make some decisions about how connected to the world we are going to be, how much we will allow it to sway us toward what feels good or toward what God says. So how will you know what should and shouldn't be in your life? You have a Holy Spirit who will convict you. And you have a Bible that shows you the standard of God. Between the two of them, you will know.

Another helpful indicator will be the fruit your life is producing. If you're too immersed in the world, then you will have worldly fruit, much like we saw earlier when Paul wrote to the church in Rome (Rom. 7:4). The natural outcomes of me-first living will ultimately come to light, and it will be hard to see a distinction between your life and that of the world. If this is you, then you likely need to hit pause and reflect on the role your feelings currently have regarding your decisions and behavior.

At some point, if we really want lasting change, then we have to stop marching to the drumbeat of the world. Many of these choices to say no to culture, to say no to our own desires, may seem abrupt, painful, and severe. I remember when I got saved at age fifteen, I immediately felt compelled to make some dramatic lifestyle changes. It wasn't easy, but I was so on fire for the Lord that I had no doubt about what I must do to follow him.

For one thing, I knew I had to get out of the high school I'd been attending. It was named Woodlawn, but everyone called it "Weedlawn," if that tells you anything. So I talked to my parents and then switched to a Christian school. It wasn't perfect, but it was definitely an improvement.

My lifestyle change also included dropping out of the four-man rock band I'd been in. I've already told you about my decision to stop listening to secular rock music, but let me explain the backstory. Prior to accepting Christ, I had lied to my parents—telling them I was spending the night at a friend's house to go with my band buddies to hear the Doobie Brothers at the Baton Rouge Civic Center downtown. Sitting there in a cloud of green smoke (remember, it was the late seventies), I about had a heart attack when the band came out and opened with "Jesus Is Just Alright." I thought, *Oh no! They're mocking Jesus—I am seriously going to hell for this!*

I also stopped dating my girlfriend at the time, Darla. I had been so excited to date her in the beginning because I loved having a cute girlfriend with that name. It reminded me of Darla on *The Little Rascals.* When I broke up with her, she was furious and had a hard time believing my reason. "Don't you trust me to respect your faith?" she asked. To which I said, "Look—I trust you just fine. It's myself I don't trust!"

I've certainly had to take other dramatic steps over the years, but those early ones stand out in my mind. As painful as they were, I've never regretted choosing my relationship with God over my friends, rock music, and girls. I took my faith seriously and took the Bible's exhortation to heart: "Come out from them and be separate, says the Lord. Touch no unclean thing, and I will receive you. . . . I will be a Father to you, and you will be my sons and daughters, says the Lord Almighty" (2 Cor. 6:17–18). What things might God be asking you to let go of?

Separation is never easy, but it is essential for your spiritual growth. Our self-sufficiency, independence, and cultural affluence often lead us to believe that our feelings determine our truth. We assume if our emotional experience is powerful enough, then it must be true. Yet if we obey our feelings rather than God's Word, it will always end badly. Bottom line: we must trust God and not ourselves. As the book of Proverbs puts it, "Trust in the

LORD with all your heart and lean not on your own understanding; in all your ways submit to him, and he will make your paths straight" (3:5–6).

The choice is yours.

Nine ———————————————————————————————

It's a Control Issue

You will never know God is all you need until He is all you have.
—Mother Teresa

It was a Thursday night, and like most nights, I went to bed pretty early. It was my habit most evenings to turn my phone off at bedtime. That night especially, I didn't want to see any more headlines or social media comments about the tragic events happening around our country. It had been another brutal week with police shootings in Minnesota and Baton Rouge, enflaming racial tensions.

When I got out of bed Friday morning, I discovered what people mean when they say their phones "blew up." I had dozens of messages, mostly from family and friends, asking me if I'd seen the latest news and what I thought of it—never a good sign first thing in the morning. At a protest in Dallas the night before, a sniper had shot and killed five police officers and injured others.

Like everyone else, I was devastated—for those officers' families, for the people involved in the previous incidents, for our nation. I knew I would have dozens of people asking me for an opinion or looking to my example on how to respond. Once again, I suspected most would not like what I had to say. Because, as saddened as I was by this latest incident, my real concern loomed much larger.

It's always easy to point fingers at the symptomatic issues and surface wounds of a situation—in this case, racism, police conduct, public response, and gun control—but underneath there's a root cause fueling all of them. The real issue—the deeper issue—is spiritual. We have walked away from God. As Dr. Martin Luther King, Jr., expressed so eloquently, "The richer we have become materially, the poorer we have become morally and spiritually. We have learned to fly the air like birds and swim the sea like fish, but we have not learned the simple art of living together as brothers."[1]

As I look at each day's headlines, I'm sad but not surprised. This is what a godless nation looks like. This is what happens when people reject God and mock his ways.

It's the natural consequence of turning our backs on God.

Truth or Consequences

Anytime tragic events and crisis-level calamities occur, many people ask, "Where is God? How could he let this happen?" But God is right where he's always been. We're the ones who have moved away from him. Our Father remains waiting for us to return so he can welcome us with open arms—just like he's always done.

Others ask, "Is this God's judgment? His punishment for what we've done?" You may disagree with me, but I don't think so. Jesus took all judgment for our sins upon himself and reconciled us to God by his death on the cross. I believe God still loves us unconditionally and desperately wants us to come home. He's always willing to extend his grace and mercy to those who seek him.

The problem, though, is that most of us don't want to. Like rebellious children, we would rather wallow around in our own indulgences than confess our sins and return to God. We are like the prodigal son in Jesus' parable; we have left the love, security, and protection of our Father to strike out on our own and then are confused by where that leads (Luke 15:11–32). But ultimately, this is our choice, and that choice comes with consequences. We can't blame the Father when we end up in a pigpen!

When we walk away from God, we leave the safety of God.

> When we walk away from God, we leave the safety of God.

He will let us, because he loves us enough to give us free will. But when we choose to leave his protection, we open ourselves up to all kinds of things. He doesn't create tragedy and instigate problems—we do. The miracle is that he's willing to use the consequences of our sin to draw us back to him and into the safety of his arms.

In the Bible we see so many generations that rejected God. You'll recall that's why God allowed the Babylonians to conquer the people of Israel. They had forsaken their God—even after he delivered them numerous times already—so he allowed them to experience the consequence. In every case, including Daniel's, the consequence was chaos.

Without God, things always turn out badly!

Changing Directions

So when we find ourselves in the midst of such chaos, what do we do? The same thing we do when we're driving and realize we've lost our way. The same solution we use when we're hiking and discover we're no longer on the right path. We turn around and seek the right direction. We turn away from the wrong direction and instead turn toward God. The good news is that he's waiting for us. He loves us and wants us back home with him, and the way back to him is the same as it's always been.

We see this way outlined in God's response to another

generation of Israelites who had rejected him. As a result of their pride and rebellion, they found themselves plagued by locusts, which led to a famine. Is there any more concise metaphor for where we are today? We have neglected our relationship with God for so long that we're now in the midst of a spiritual and moral famine with no relief in sight. No relief, that is, until we do the same four things that God told the Israelites to do:

> If my people, who are called by my name, will humble themselves
> and pray and seek my face and turn from their wicked ways, then
> I will hear from heaven, and I will forgive their sin and will heal
> their land. (2 Chron. 7:14)

Yes, the healing of our land begins with us. Notice the four items mentioned here.

First, we must humble ourselves. Humility provides the foundation for true repentance. So many Christians respond to others today with arrogance and anger. I'm often embarrassed at the way their responses only pour more fuel onto cultural fires that are already burning. If we want to return to God and restore our nation, then we must begin by humbling ourselves.

Instead of pointing our fingers at others, we can only point at ourselves. Our anger must not be allowed to go unchecked. Humility has to rule in all we do. We've been an arrogant nation and assumed we know what's best. And many of us have even assumed that God is on our side—instead of the other way around. In the throes of cultural chaos, we will either choose humility or humiliation. Instead of writing critical comments and quoting verses on blogs and online news sites, we should be on our knees before God.

We must also show humility and compassion in how we relate to others. We don't know what they've been through. We can't read their minds or see into their souls like God can. I remember seeing an African American reporter describing to his son how he should react if he is ever driving and gets pulled over by law enforcement. I wept as I absorbed this man's experience and all he had been through and therefore felt compelled to download to his son. This experience caused me to respond more compassionately to everyone around me, to remember that I'm no better than anyone else, especially those who consistently battle prejudice and injustice.

If we're serious about repentance, then humility must envelop all we say and do—with God first and then with others.

Next, we must pray. As I read on a bumper sticker, "Prayer should always be our first response—not our last resort!" It's a shame it takes tragedy to return us to prayer. Throughout the Bible, we're told to be people of prayer who depend on God for everything.

> If we're serious about repentance, then humility must envelop all we say and do— with God first and then with others.

But even if we do pray as a last resort, God still responds right away! How cool is that? We're told, "Draw near to God and He will draw near to you. Cleanse your hands, you sinners; and purify your hearts, you double-minded" (James 4:8 NKJV).

Prayer is not informing God about our realities. It's aligning our hearts with his realities. If we are seated with Christ in heavenly places, like Paul talked about in Ephesians 2:6, then prayer is that place next to Jesus where our perspective changes. Prayer is the place where we cry out to God, *I need you!* which brings us to our third instruction for returning to God.

We must seek his face. Now, before you say you've never seen God's face, keep in mind that this simply means his character.

Making our way back to him, we need to seek his heart, his ways, his standards. When we seek God in this way, we realize just how far we've strayed and its impact on our lives. As we seek God, we must pray and ask the Holy Spirit to show us those areas of compromise and convict us. Like the psalmist we pray, "Search me, God, and know

> Prayer is not informing God about our realities. It's aligning our hearts with his realities.

my heart; test me and know my anxious thoughts. See if there is any offensive way in me, and lead me in the way everlasting" (Ps. 139:23–24). Once God shows us, then it's time for the fourth and final part.

We must turn. I love the simplicity of this word: *turn.* God doesn't require us to make up for our mistakes in any way. He doesn't want a price. He just says for us to turn back—from our ways to his ways. It's that simple.

That's what the word *repentance* literally means: to turn around. And as a nation, we need to repent for the many ways we have turned from God: for our disregard for human life, as evidenced by our abortion, violence, and racism; for our sexual immorality, as seen in our promiscuity, pornography, and pursuit of personal pleasure; and for failing to serve those in need—the poor, the homeless, and the sick.

When we stop pointing a finger at others and instead pray, *Lord, change me,* then three things will happen. First, we will hear from heaven. God will not fail to respond to the cry of our hearts. We must let him know that we need his kingdom to come and his will to be done here on earth just as it is in heaven. There's a reason this request is central to the Lord's Prayer, the model of prayer that Jesus taught his disciples (Matt. 6:9–13).

When we pray and seek God's response, he will forgive us our sins and grant us a fresh start. He will heal our hearts and remove the layers of shame, perversion, anger, distrust, and pain. When we pray with fervency and sincerity, then we can trust God to do the rest. It likely won't happen overnight (although it can!), but we can rest in the confidence of knowing we have returned to the shelter of his wings, the arms of the Almighty.

Have It Your Way

Okay, Chris, you might be thinking, *if repentance comes down to those four steps, then why is it so hard? Why aren't more people turning back toward God? Why is it so hard for me to return to God sometimes?*

I'm glad you asked, because this is the real heart of the problem. Deep down inside, we like control. We like things to go "our way." We like doing things ourselves, so we can have them the way we want them to be. There's so much pride in our individuality that we're still singing, "I did it my way!"

Allow me to confess something to you: I'm a control freak. I like things done my way. I'm living proof of the saying, "As long as everything goes exactly like I want it, I'm totally flexible." But in my battle for control over the years, I've also discovered the more tightly I hang on, the less control I actually have.

When I first began ministry as a young single adult, I assumed that to be a good pastor I should get married. Each of the pastors I admired had been married for years to a lovely woman, and so I thought I needed to hurry up and find one too. With this mindset, I dated—a lot—but I might as well have been conducting job interviews! Instead of dating and enjoying a young woman's company in a natural way, I added pressure because I was so eager to find "the right one" to be my wife. No wonder I scared 'em all away!

Finally, I began to realize my efforts weren't working. I was tired of trying and thought it was time for a break. I told God, *You called me into ministry, and when I answered, you led the way. If you want me to marry, then I'm going to trust you to do the same thing. It's not happening right now for me. So I'm going to relax and believe that when the time is right, you'll let me know if I'm to marry and to whom.*

The next month I met Tammy.

Maybe we hit it off because I wasn't trying so hard. I could enjoy getting to know her without worrying about whether we would marry. It's amazing how when you let something go, it seems to pop back up in your life. Again and again, I've had to learn this lesson. But it's true. It's better to give up

> It's better to give up and trust God than to cling tight and try to control everything.

and trust God than to cling tight and try to control everything.

You might not be surprised to learn that the Babylonian leaders in Daniel's day could come across like control freaks—at least to me they do. In perhaps the most famous story from the book of Daniel, he's thrown into the lions' den and emerges unharmed. But do you remember why he was tossed in with all the big cats? Let's take a look:

> Then they said to the king, "Daniel, who is one of the exiles from Judah, pays no attention to you, Your Majesty, or to the decree you put in writing. He still prays three times a day." When the king heard this, he was greatly distressed; he was determined to rescue Daniel and made every effort until sundown to save him.
>
> Then the men went as a group to King Darius and said to him, "Remember, Your Majesty, that according to the law of the

Medes and Persians no decree or edict that the king issues can be changed."

So the king gave the order, and they brought Daniel and threw him into the lions' den. The king said to Daniel, "May your God, whom you serve continually, rescue you!"

A stone was brought and placed over the mouth of the den, and the king sealed it with his own signet ring and with the rings of his nobles, so that Daniel's situation might not be changed. Then the king returned to his palace and spent the night without eating and without any entertainment being brought to him. And he could not sleep.

At the first light of dawn, the king got up and hurried to the lions' den. When he came near the den, he called to Daniel in an anguished voice, "Daniel, servant of the living God, has your God, whom you serve continually, been able to rescue you from the lions?"

Daniel answered, "May the king live forever! My God sent his angel, and he shut the mouths of the lions. They have not hurt me, because I was found innocent in his sight. Nor have I ever done any wrong before you, Your Majesty."

The king was overjoyed and gave orders to lift Daniel out of the den. And when Daniel was lifted from the den, no wound was found on him, because he had trusted in his God. (Dan. 6:13–23)

King Darius clearly liked Daniel—he was reluctant to throw him in the lions' den, didn't sleep all night, and was overjoyed when Daniel emerged unhurt. But Darius fell victim to his own authority, along with the manipulation of his court leaders, who were jealous of Daniel. Darius had appointed 120 satraps, or court officials, and then chosen three administrators to lead them all, one of whom was Daniel. When the other lieutenants saw how highly the king thought of Daniel, they realized their own positions were in jeopardy.

Consequently, they devised a plan that rather ingeniously played on the king's own prideful ego. These influencers convinced Darius to issue a decree forbidding everyone in the kingdom from praying or worshipping anything or anyone except the king. Those who didn't obey this decree would face certain death as catnip for a pride of hungry lions. Without thinking through the consequences of this decree, the king unwittingly allowed Daniel to be set up. And rather than change his decree—and risk losing face with his subjects—Darius went along with it, all the while hoping Daniel would survive, which of course he did because God protected Daniel.

My fear is that too often we as Christians end up acting more like Darius and his court leaders than like Daniel. Like Darius, we feel obligated to follow the crowd, go with the flow, and not upset the boat. We don't want to look weak or foolish in front of others, so we subtly compromise our faith, refusing to speak up. Like Darius's court officials, we try to control our own lives and manipulate people and events to work the way we want them to work.

Rarely does this go well.

And it always moves us further away from God.

Remote Control

Perhaps there's no better example of someone attempting to control his own life before surrendering to God than Jacob. You'll recall that Jacob was the grandson of Abraham and the son of Isaac. And, honestly, even from the moment he was born, Jacob tried to control the situation. He was a twin and, apparently seeing his brother, Esau, leaving their mother's womb first, Jacob grabbed his brother's heel! *Hey, you're not getting that firstborn son's blessing. I want it!* In fact, Jacob's very name means "trickster," "supplanter," or "heel grabber."

This desire to control outcomes quickly became a theme in Jacob's life. He fought to get ahead his whole life. With some help from his mom, Jacob stole his brother's birthright—exploiting his brother's hunger in a vulnerable moment and then tricking their father into giving Jacob his blessing.

Knowing how angry his brother and father were, Jacob then ran away to stay with his uncle Laban, where Jacob fell in love with Rachel. Despite agreeing to his uncle's conditions in order to marry her, Jacob got a taste of his own medicine and found himself deceived and tricked into marrying the wrong woman, Rachel's sister Leah.

Later on, he finally married Rachel, but Jacob still tried to control his life. In fact, he was especially famous for wrestling with God, who was disguised as an angel taking human form, while trying to face up to his past. Jacob refused to let go of his divine opponent until he received a blessing, which he received along with a limp and a name change from Jacob to Israel, from "heel-grabbing controller" to "one who has wrestled and overcome." Jacob spent his whole life fighting for a future God already had planned for him.

Too many of us are doing the same thing—fighting for a future God already has planned. God will let us try to control our own lives, but our efforts will fail. In fact, old Jacob would be the first to tell us that when our lives aren't turning out the way we hoped, we should just let God have control.

You see, just before that life-changing wrestling match with God, Jacob had run out of options. Running away yet again—this time from his father-in-law—he discovered his brother, Esau, was chasing him. As a strategy to mislead Esau, Jacob divided his family, servants, and possessions into two camps. He sent the remaining members of his family away and decided he would face Esau alone in a final showdown. All the problems in his life were converging and reaching a boiling point. His commitment to control had reached a climax. One way or another, his life had to change.

The night before his unavoidable meeting with the brother he had cheated, Jacob found himself confronted with a more urgent opponent. Let's pick up the story in Genesis 32:

> This left Jacob all alone in the camp, and a man came and wrestled with him until the dawn began to break. When the man saw that he would not win the match, he touched Jacob's hip and wrenched it out of its socket. (vv. 24–25 NLT)

Jacob's opponent wasn't just a former WWF contender who wandered by. This was God in disguise. God wanted Jacob to stop trusting in his own power, and so he intentionally took away Jacob's natural ability by wounding his hip. Jacob would be forced to rely on God's ability and strength if he wanted to survive.

It's a lesson we all need to learn today. So often we rely on what we think we can control for our sense of security. We put our trust in money, in our job titles, in our bank accounts, in our intelligence, in who we know. But eventually none of these are enough

> If we're going to make it, then we need a new strength.

and we end up exhausted. Trouble hits and we run away, only to discover there's no escape. Our lives reach a climax of events where we must make a decision. If we're going to make it, then we need a new strength.

Jesus made it clear where help can be found: "Come to me, all you who are weary and burdened, and I will give you rest. Take my yoke upon you and learn from me, for I am gentle and humble in heart, and you will find rest for your souls" (Matt. 11:28–29).

Notice he said, "Take my yoke"—which means we'll have to let go of our own. In other words, stop doing it your way and try my way—it's much lighter.

Like eagles that can fly higher without flapping their wings, we can soar to new heights if we let God empower us.

And we not only receive a new strength and power when we surrender and allow God to control our lives; we, like Jacob, also receive a new identity. Notice at the end of his heated wrestling match with God, a very important conversation takes place:

> "What is your name?" the man asked.
>
> He replied, "Jacob."
>
> "Your name will no longer be Jacob," the man told him. "From now on you will be called Israel, because you have fought with God and with men and have won." (Gen. 32:27–28 NLT)

First, God made Jacob admit who he was, what he had been his whole life, a "trickster" and a "heel-grabber"—a control freak. But then he gave Jacob a new name, an identity based on his willingness to surrender and cling to God and God alone. He would no longer be the trickster known as Jacob; from then on he would be known as Israel, a prince with God (Gen. 32:28 KJV).

God doesn't see what you are but what you can become. He doesn't see actualities; he sees possibilities. Your Creator sees greatness in you that you don't even see in yourself.

Give God the control of your life, and he'll give you a new name!

Blessed U-Turns

The last part of Jacob's transformation after surrendering to God involved blessing. "'Please tell me your name,' Jacob said. 'Why do you want to know my name?' the man replied. Then he blessed Jacob there" (Gen. 32:29 NLT). The word we usually translate as *blessed* in this verse means "happy." God made Jacob happy here, not with a temporary, feel-good type of happiness but with an internal joy that would endure the rest of his life.

We see this same idea of blessing in the Beatitudes from Jesus' Sermon on the Mount. There he listed nine "Blessed are . . ." statements and indicated what we receive when we're willing to seek God first instead of our own way. Let's look at one of these statements that makes our point. Jesus said, "Blessed are those who hunger and thirst for righteousness, for they will be filled" (Matt. 5:6). When we long for God and his holiness over our own ideas of what is right or what will make us happy, we will be filled. Or, in my paraphrase, blessed are those who make a U-turn and come home to God.

Jacob learned the hard way that brokenness precedes breakthrough. We cannot be who God intends us to be and at the same time hold on to what we think we should be. The most positive, affirming, life-changing verb in the Bible is *repent*. Too often when we hear this word today, it has a negative connotation related to judgment and condemnation. But it should convey the exact opposite: freedom, restoration, new life.

Remember—God isn't looking for perfection. He's looking for humility and honesty about our need for him, our brokenness. The Bible tells us God is especially attracted to a repentant heart: "My sacrifice, O God, is a broken spirit; a broken and contrite heart you, God, will not despise" (Ps. 51:17).

If we want to stand strong in a bow-down culture, then we must be willing to lose control. Jacob fought hard for the life he wanted, but the harder he fought, the further away he was. Even up until the end, he was always struggling, grappling and wrestling with God and refusing to give up. Many times we work so hard to keep our lives together when God simply wants us to quit fighting him. "If you try to hang on to your life, you will lose it. But if you give up your life for my sake and for the sake of the Good News, you will save it" (Mark 8:35 NLT). You'll never know all that your life can be until you hand it over to the One who gave you life.

As you'll recall, we started this chapter with a heavy point about the tragic, devastating state of our world today. In the middle of such crises, people often ask me what they can do. I suspect they're expecting me to reply with something like "pray" or some specific way they can contribute money or resources. While those are excellent responses, what I tell people most often is simply to check the direction of their hearts.

> You'll never know all that your life can be until you hand it over to the One who gave you life.

I rarely use the word *repent*, but that's basically what I mean. Because if we're seeking God first, with humility and a willingness to surrender our controlling nature, then he will restore us, one by one, church by church, community by community, state by state, and nation by nation. We simply cannot change on our own.

God is our only hope.

Part 4

Culture's Greatest Culprit: Unfocused and Busy Lives

Where Is My Focus?

Ten

MY DAYS ARE NUMBERED

The time is always right to do what is right.

—MARTIN LUTHER KING, JR.

At the hospital with Keith—not good," the text read.

I had just arrived at our church for an all-staff meeting when I received this text from Layne Schranz, one of our pastors. He was at a nearby hospital checking on Keith Lindsey, another one of our pastors and a valued member of our team. Keith had been battling multiple myeloma, cancer of the blood, but last we had heard his prognosis was good because the prescribed treatment had been effective. We had been praying for Keith and were excited about him coming home from the hospital and getting to be back at church with us. As I texted with Layne, however, it was clear Keith had taken a turn for the worse. At first his doctors had been confident Keith's body could handle the ongoing treatment, but this no longer seemed to be the case.

"Do I need to come?" I texted to Layne.

"No, I think he's fine."

Minutes later Layne texted, "He's not doing well all of a sudden!"

"What happened?" I asked. "Keep me posted."

Less than ten minutes later: "He's gone."

"What?!!" I texted back. "I'll be right there."

And just like that, our beloved friend and associate pastor was in heaven. I've been in ministry for thirty-three years and, sadly, have experienced many situations like this. But never had I seen a situation pivot so quickly, without warning. We thought Keith was out of the woods and on his way home. And he was, only he went to his eternal home, not the one here on earth.

Once again I was reminded, as I always am when experiencing or leading others through this kind of loss, just how short life can be on this side of eternity. The truth is, our days here on earth are numbered. As much as we may not like keeping this fact in mind, remembering that our days are numbered can keep us focused on making the most of the time we have.

Handwriting

What does this have to do with the book of Daniel? What does this have to do with living a stand-up life in a bow-down world? What correlation is there between our time on earth and the shifting of our culture? Everything!

Remember, the book of Daniel is in the prophecy section of Scripture in the Old Testament. It not only tells us stories of what happened to Daniel and the people of Israel during their captivity in Babylon, but it also serves as a prophetic picture of our lives today. It warns, informs, and encourages believers to live a godly life in an ungodly culture, a field guide for living in the last days.

Let me remind you about what we've covered so far. In part 1 of this book we explored how the Babylonian culture attacked the identity of their Hebrew prisoners of war. The hedonistic captors tried to rename them, tame them, and claim them. Still today, our identities are the battleground for culture's attack. In part 2 we saw how Daniel and his friends were challenged on who and what they would and would not worship—which remains culture's greatest test. Pride, culture's greatest sin, was the subject of part 3.

And now in part 4, I want to focus on what I believe to be culture's greatest illusion—the twin culprits of deception and distraction. These culture-colored glasses cause us to fail tests, worship false idols, live in pride, and errantly view our time in this life. I'm convinced the order of the book of Daniel is just as prophetic as its core message. As we look at another chapter describing Daniel's time in Babylon, it's clear God still speaks to us today just as he warned King Belshazzar. Here's how it went down:

King Belshazzar gave a great banquet for a thousand of his nobles and drank wine with them. While Belshazzar was drinking his wine, he gave orders to bring in the gold and silver goblets that Nebuchadnezzar his father had taken from the temple in Jerusalem, so that the king and his nobles, his wives and his concubines might drink from them. So they brought in the gold goblets that had been taken from the temple of God in Jerusalem, and the king and his nobles, his wives and his concubines drank from them. As they drank the wine, they praised the gods of gold and silver, of bronze, iron, wood and stone.

Suddenly the fingers of a human hand appeared and wrote on the plaster of the wall, near the lampstand in the royal palace. The king watched the hand as it wrote. His face turned pale and he was so frightened that his legs became weak and his knees were knocking.

The king summoned the enchanters, astrologers and diviners. Then he said to these wise men of Babylon, "Whoever reads this writing and tells me what it means will be clothed in purple and have a gold chain placed around his neck, and he will be made the third highest ruler in the kingdom." (Dan. 5:1–7)

The king's wise men came in, and they couldn't translate the strange writing that had mysteriously appeared from the floating hand. This sounds like something out of an Edgar Allan Poe story—but this actually happened! I've always wondered if this was a giant-sized hand or just a regular-sized one. And did it look wispy and ghostlike or was it more like "Thing" on *The Addams Family*? Whatever it looked like, it sure shook up old Belshazzar! His knees were knocking, and yours and mine probably would have been too. When his consultants failed to translate the writing, the queen remembered Daniel and had him brought in.

> So Daniel was brought before the king, and the king said to him, "Are you Daniel, one of the exiles my father the king brought from Judah? I have heard that the spirit of the gods is in you and that you have insight, intelligence and outstanding wisdom. The wise men and enchanters were brought before me to read this writing and tell me what it means, but they could not explain it. Now I have heard that you are able to give interpretations and to solve difficult problems. If you can read this writing and tell me what it means, you will be clothed in purple and have a gold chain placed around your neck, and you will be made the third highest ruler in the kingdom." (Dan. 5:13–16)

Daniel came in and assessed the situation, and he essentially told Belshazzar, "Look, you can keep your gifts. I'll tell you what this message says, but you probably won't like it." We're told that this new king reminded Daniel of the previous king, Belshazzar's father, Nebuchadnezzar, who didn't listen to God's warnings either and went insane for seven years before he repented and God restored him. Like father, like son, right?

Daniel told Belshazzar that, like his dad, he had allowed his pride and arrogance to get in the way:

Instead, you have set yourself up against the Lord of heaven. You had the goblets from his temple brought to you, and you and your nobles, your wives and your concubines drank wine from them. You praised the gods of silver and gold, of bronze, iron, wood and stone, which cannot see or hear or understand. But you did not honor the God who holds in his hand your life and all your ways. Therefore he sent the hand that wrote the inscription. (Dan. 5:23–24)

Like many phrases and verses derived from the Bible, the saying "the handwriting is on the wall" has become a common colloquialism meaning "imminent doom." It's like a warning label stuck to the side of your life. When the handwriting's on the wall, it means everyone can see that disaster is about to happen. Something heavy is about to drop.

In fact, if we look closely at Daniel's translation of what was written, we can see both a warning of coming punishment for Belshazzar and several key principles about how we are to live in the last days to avoid a similar punishment in eternity. Remember, Daniel is a prophetic book, and the handwriting remains on the wall for us today. Our lives are slipping through our hands like water, and if we don't slow down and refocus on what matters most, we will lose something precious and irreplaceable. But it's not too late—yet. So let's spend the rest of this chapter unpacking the first principle and then examine the others in the two remaining chapters in part 4.

Your Days Are Numbered

"This is the inscription that was written: MENE, MENE, TEKEL, PARSIN" (Dan. 5:25). Keep in mind that this message was supernatural in origin; while some scholars believe these words are

Aramaic in origin, God basically created his own language for this inscription, knowing that his man Dan would be the only one capable of translating it. Daniel's translation—and ours—zeroes in on the fuller meaning behind the three words, the first of which is repeated: "Here is what these words mean: *Mene*: God has numbered the days of your reign and brought it to an end" (Dan. 5:26). The Hebrew word that Daniel chose for his translation of God's message, *mene*, literally meant "numbered." And for added emphasis—it's repeated.

> Only following God and living for him provides the kind of deep significance we crave and were created to enjoy.

It's a caution flag that continues to flutter today in the shifting winds of our culture, and its message is simple: *Don't forget that your days are numbered.* But somehow, that's exactly what we often do. We live like there's no tomorrow, literally, and we only want to "eat, drink and be merry" (Luke 12:19). But God's Word tells us that "people are destined to die once, and after that to face judgment" (Heb. 9:27). And the truth is, death could happen at any time.

Belshazzar's greatest sin was how he wasted his life. He didn't realize that his life was short in the context of eternity. If he had grasped this truth, then he would have chosen to live for God instead of himself. When we realize that our days are numbered, then we realize the need to make them count. Only following God and living for him provides the kind of deep significance we crave and were created to enjoy.

If we lived with the truth that we have a finite amount of time, a limited number of days, then we would make better decisions. Anytime you think you have more of something than you need, you tend to waste it. It's just the logic of human nature. If you have plenty of food in your pantry, cupboard, and fridge, it's hard to imagine being hungry. If there's lots of money in your bank account, then you feel like you'll always have enough. But when you're down to your last box of crackers or last dollar, suddenly these things become precious. You no longer take them for granted. When we recognize our limitations, we tend to make the most of our lives.

This truth jumped out at us a few years ago when we did a series at our church called 30 Days to Live. Basically, we asked people how they would assess their lifestyles, relationships, and daily choices if they were told they only had a month left to live. It remains a powerful, revealing exercise. What would you start doing if you only had thirty days left? What would you stop doing if that was all the time remaining in your life? How would you spend those limited, precious few weeks? Who would you want to spend them with?

> When we recognize our limitations, we tend to make the most of our lives.

As part of the series, I interviewed several people whose doctors had told them they had a short amount of time to live. These were real testimonies of people who had literally been given a "death date" that was quickly approaching. With this kind of urgency front and center, they shared a very different perspective on their priorities than most people have.

These individuals revealed how so many things that used to matter suddenly didn't seem important at all anymore. And many of the things they used to not have time for suddenly became part of every remaining day. Because they had a limited amount of time, they knew they couldn't waste a moment. When we live with this perspective, we can face the shifts of culture with a different attitude—one of clarity and focus on what matters most, one that sets aside the distractions this world offers and keeps our eyes on God.

If Belshazzar had this kind of perspective, then the last thing he probably would have been doing was partying and mocking God. But if we jump to the end of his story, we see his time ran out.

> Then at Belshazzar's command, Daniel was clothed in purple, a gold chain was placed around his neck, and he was proclaimed the third highest ruler in the kingdom.
>
> That very night Belshazzar, king of the Babylonians, was slain, and Darius the Mede took over the kingdom, at the age of sixty-two. (Dan. 5:29–31)

It was too late for Belshazzar, but if you're reading this right now, then you still have time. Time to change and realign your life around what God wants. To be the person he created you to be.

To stand apart from the cultural chaos.
To live for your God.
To heed his message.

Live Like You're Dying

If you want to stand strong in a bow-down world, if you want to put God first in your life, you need to start right now.

First, *choose to live every day with a sense of purpose and urgency.* Live as though you have limited time—because you do!

Let's revisit the questions we asked in our church's 30 Days to Live series. Just think for a moment: What activities would you eliminate if you lived with the end in mind? Less time surfing online? Fewer pics posted on Instagram? Not as much overtime at work? If you knew you only had thirty days to live, what would you stop doing and what would you start doing instead?

Whenever I think about living with a sense of urgent purpose, my father-in-law, Billy, always comes to mind. He knew how to make every single moment count for eternity. The man was literally on his deathbed, but he was still using his time in this life to influence God's kingdom. Billy had more than three hundred visitors come to see him during the last few weeks of his life. And he definitely ministered more to them than they ministered to him. Ministering to others was life for him. So he spent time with each person, talking and praying for them, encouraging them. He remains a role model for me in making the most of the time we're given.

Next, *put first things first.* Make sure your priorities really are front and center each day. Don't put off focusing on the people and principles that matter most to you. Regularly check on how you're spending your time, and reorder your schedule as needed. And, yes, I know this is easier said than done! Putting first things first means you must stop the constant push and pull for more. What the world and others around you consider urgent is rarely truly urgent. What matters most for God's kingdom, for making the most of the life he's given you—that's what's urgent.

The solution is simple but an ongoing battle: you must say no! When you're tempted to hold a grudge against a loved one or feel sorry for yourself, then you must think, *No! Ain't nobody got time for that. With the days I have left, I'm going to live my life for God, for what matters the most to me.* The psalmist said, "Teach us to number our days and recognize how few they are; help us to spend them as we should" (Ps. 90:12 TLB).

The secret to focusing on first things is maintaining order, keeping our priorities in the right sequence. Our perspective on order determines our capacity. Jesus talked about this principle in his famous sermon:

So do not worry, saying, "What shall we eat?" or "What shall we drink?" or "What shall we wear?" For the pagans run after all these things, and your heavenly Father knows that you need them. But seek first his kingdom and his righteousness, and all these things will be given to you as well. (Matt. 6:31–33)

Jesus is saying that more will happen, more will get done, when we put him first in our lives. When we keep order in our daily lives, then we keep our priorities clear. Order communicates priority. As Christians, we can be really busy doing a lot of good stuff for the wrong reasons. We slip into a mind-set of doing more so that we can feel like we're closer to God or better Christians. But if we're not spending one-on-one, intimate time with God each day and then acting out of the overflow of that relationship rather than the other way around, then we have lost sight of why we're doing all that we're doing. One thing must come first and lead to the other. The order can't be flipped.

Whatever we put in first place becomes the organizing principle for the other parts of our lives. Think of it like an outline for those papers you had to write in school. When you focus on your guiding principle, it automatically takes care of many other decisions. We're told, "In all your ways submit to him. . . . Honor the LORD with your wealth, with the firstfruits of all your crops; then your barns will be filled to overflowing, and your vats will brim over with new wine" (Prov. 3:6, 9–10). This passage may be about money, but the principle is true for all things.

> As Christians we can be really busy doing a lot of good stuff for the wrong reasons.

One of my favorite illustrations of this principle came from a business seminar I attended in Colorado many years ago. It made a huge impact on me, so I often include it whenever I teach on the way order influences the rest of our lives. I take two gallon-sized glass jars and fill one about three-quarters full with the little gravel that goes into aquariums. Then I'll have about seven or eight big rocks at least the size of my fist or larger.

The gravel represents all the "little things" in our day—texting, shopping, waiting in line at Starbucks, watching TV, ordering from Amazon, all the stuff we do on any given day. And the bigger rocks represent our main priorities: our relationship with God, our relationships with our spouses and kids, our commitment to exercise and having healthy bodies, our dedication to our careers, to serving others, to friendships—whatever our other priorities happen to be.

The funny thing, though, is that when you try to put your "priority rocks" into the jar that's already close to full of gravel, there's not enough room. All your priorities can't be squeezed into your life when it's full of daily "gravel." But when the priority rocks are placed in the jar first, and then the gravel is poured on top, they all fit—there may even be room left over.

Order matters! When you make sure you put your priorities first, the rest of your life will wrap around and fill in the gaps. But it won't work the other way. You have to put priorities ahead of the little stuff.

And what should be our greatest priority? Jesus gave us the answer: "But seek first his kingdom and his righteousness, and all these things will be given to you as well" (Matt. 6:33). Most of us know the importance of ordering our lives around our principles and priorities, but we let the culture and so many other distractions squeeze them out. But our days are limited. How we spend our time matters. Let's reorder our lives so we live on purpose every day.

The Time Is Now

As a pastor, I do a lot of funerals, and while I try to personalize each service to honor the person and comfort the family as much as possible, my message is fundamentally the same for each one. I call it the "heavenly perspective." This is the choice you make to try and see things from an eternal perspective when your experience here on earth hurts so much. The heavenly perspective reminds you that one day it will all make sense. One day this loss will no longer hurt this way. One day your troubles will fade away, and there will be no more problems.

Now, I realize it's hard to have this perspective without having been to heaven yet. But that's why we have testimonies in the Bible from some who have. In Scripture we find accounts from three people who saw heaven. Jesus, of course, talked more about heaven than anyone else, which makes sense because he lived there before he came to earth. Heaven was his first home. Jesus said that we don't need to be afraid of what happens to our physical bodies. The tragedy of dying is not losing your physical body but missing heaven if you didn't choose God here on earth.

When Jesus encouraged people during his ministry, it was always with heaven and never with the now. In the book of John, for example, he said, "Do not let your hearts be troubled. You believe in God; believe also in me. My Father's house has many rooms" (John 14:1–2). He told us not to let our hearts be troubled, not because there's an answer on the way, but because of heaven. Christ offers more than a better now; he offers us the best place ever.

The apostle Paul also saw heaven in a vision. When his enemies threatened to kill him, Paul basically said, "Would you? Please?" He wrote, "For to me, to live is Christ and to die is gain" (Phil. 1:21). It was actually a dilemma for Paul to continue living, considering that he knew heaven was his final home. He considered his options the ultimate win-win: he could live for Christ on earth or die and be with Christ in heaven.

John the Beloved also gave us his perspective on heaven in Revelation. He wrote, "He will wipe every tear from their eyes. There will be no more death or mourning or crying or pain, for the old order of things has passed away" (21:4). John knew that God created us to be with him in heaven. That's why we can never find ultimate satisfaction here on earth.

Some people would rather hear me talk about making everything work here on earth in this life rather than keeping our eyes on what is to come in heaven, but that's not the way God's plan works. God's plan has always been a rescue mission, to bring us home to heaven. All throughout the Bible, we're told to set our minds on things above and not on earthly things. In the "Faith Hall of Fame" passage in Hebrews, we're reminded that although the saints before us experienced many amazing miracles, nothing compares with their ultimate reward: being with God in heaven. "These were all commended for their faith, yet none of them received what had been promised, since God had planned something better . . ." (11:39–40).

> Christ offers more than a better now; he offers us the best place ever.

My friend, eternity is closer than you can possibly imagine. Our days are numbered. Like Belshazzar, today might be our last day in this life. I pray that it's not, but we all need to consider the realistic possibility, especially in the world we live in today. One of the worst things we can do is put off living for God until it's too late.

Many people live in what I call the "when . . . then" syndrome. We make living our lives deliberately conditional on some future goal or event. We refuse to make the most of today because we're waiting on something that may or may not happen. We say things like:

> One day when I get married, then I will be happy.
> One day when I get the right home,
> then I'll lead a small group.
> One day when I get out of debt, then I'll start to tithe.
> One day when the kids are grown, then
> we'll work on our marriage.

But "one day" has to be today! It's too easy to live in a time other than the right-now. Paul reminds us in his letter to the church in Corinth, "I tell you, now is the time of God's favor, now is the day of salvation" (2 Cor. 6:2). Now is the time for us to get right with God. His favor is now. His salvation is now.

Don't wait; don't put it off.

Do it *now*.

Eleven

My Life Is Unbalanced

The wisdom of life consists in the elimination of nonessentials. . . . Besides the noble art of getting things
done, there is a nobler art of leaving things undone.

—Lin Yutang

O ur bathroom scale sits right next to the toilet in our master
bathroom. I see it every day, and it never fails to invite me
to step on so it can mock me with a higher number than last time.
It's easy to hate that scale and how it reminds me of all my bad
choices—those bowls of ice cream before bedtime, extra ranch
dressing on my salad, and a third helping of my wife's lasagna.
I've never been obese, at least not by my own assessment, but I've
never been in tip-top shape either. I jokingly tell people, "I'm not
in shape—I'm in *a* shape. You know, round is a shape!"

I'm certainly no authority on weight loss or physical fitness,
so I won't continue sharing this little battle with you. But I do
know something about weighing our time—because God's Word
speaks about it a lot. We're responsible for how we spend the limited number of days we have here on earth. And when we weigh
our lives and consider how we've spent those days, what will the
scales show?

Almost everyone says they don't spend their time the way they
want. How many times a day have you heard or been asked, "Hey,

how are you?" Of course, the most common response is, "Busy." There was a time when "I'm fine" was the usual response, but I rarely hear it anymore, because everyone is so quick to say "busy." It's become accepted in our culture, almost like a badge of honor proclaiming, "Yes, I've been busy working so hard so that I can be busy all the time—that's just the kind of hardworking, industrious, busy person I am!"

But this is incredibly dangerous.

Because busy is never better.

The Biggest Loser

You'll recall we left Daniel translating the mysterious words written on King Belshazzar's wall by the spooky hand. The first word, *mene*, told us our days are numbered. This should shift us toward a more focused and heavenly perspective as we live out those days. Now let's look at the second word from the handwriting on the wall, *tekel*, which literally means "weighed." As Daniel explained to the king, "*Tekel*: You have been weighed on the scales and found wanting" (Dan. 5:27). In other words, not only are our days numbered, but we are also responsible for how we spend them.

> Busy is never better.

If your life was weighed today, what would the scales say? Would your life be found wanting? If we looked at how you use your time, would it be out of balance with your life's priorities? What would your spouse say? How about your kids? Your friends?

Convicted? I am too.

These are hard questions to face. In fact, many times my response is summed up by this verse: "My days go by faster than a runner; they fly away without my seeing any joy" (Job 9:25 NCV). We all know being out of balance isn't good for us. We all know there are other things that are more important to us than working late, surfing Facebook, or shopping online. We all know that no one on their deathbed wishes they could have spent another hour at Costco.

So why do we do it to ourselves? For starters, I'm convinced we have too many choices. Choices of places to eat, things to do, social media platforms to check in on. Choices about where to go, who to go with, what to wear, when to shop. Choices about what kind of store to browse, what flavor of mustard to buy, and what size container to buy it in. Hundreds of choices—*every day.*

Part of this problem stems from the enormous social pressure we feel to say yes to things that we really don't want to do or have time to do. But we don't want to disappoint other people—family members, coworkers, bosses, friends, and neighbors. And don't forget the social pressure to "keep up with the Joneses." Someone gets something, and we talk ourselves into believing that we have to have it too. We want to belong, to fit in, to be seen as successful (or more successful) than everyone around us.

And then there's the whole financial doctrine of today that says, "You can have it *all* and have it all *now.*" You might be too young to know about purchasing something on layaway. Instead of putting something on credit, you'd put it on hold (or layaway) at the store, make payments on it over weeks or months, and then when it was fully paid, you'd go pick it up. Today we do the very opposite. We pick it out at the store, put it on credit, bring it home, use it up, and years later, we're still making payments on it. Then we wonder why we never feel caught up on our finances!

If we listen to the many voices of our culture, then we also believe we can do it all—that there's no limit to our abilities. So we go without sleep, nutrition, rest, reflection, learning, playing, relating, praying—and then wonder why we feel so stressed.

Our bodies, minds, and souls get conditioned to run on empty, exhausted beyond the limits at which we were created to live.

We can't live under this kind of pressure.

We weren't intended to.

Stress Tests

I could spend the rest of this book giving you reasons why we're all so stressed and unbalanced in our lives. And I don't mean that I have it all figured out. I'll let you in on yet another little secret about me: I get really burned out every year around May. It's usually right after I've been preaching for about four months straight, followed by weeks of traveling and speaking at conferences in the spring, and topped off by the big Easter services we have each year.

I reach a tipping point, and it's not tilting in a good direction. By the end of May, I'm running on fumes, just scraping by. When I was younger, I used to push through fueled by adrenaline. I thought I had no choice in the matter and told myself things like, "We're building a church here—they need me. This is what God has called me to do. I must do it!"

Maybe you think you have no choice right now either. This is just how life is. And actually, you're right: this will always be how things are with the lifestyle society has convinced us we must have. The lifestyle that revolves around big houses, nice cars, the latest designer fashions, expensive hobbies, and, of course, everything our kids want. Day in and day out, the weight is crushing. We all have these demands—obligations and responsibilities that force us to spend our time in wrong ways.

I get it. It's tempting to think it's a time-management problem. But you've probably already realized, likely in frustration, that it's not a matter of squeezing everything in; the bottom line is that all you're doing right now is never going to fit in a balanced way.

We've so packed our lives full that even if we fill our jars with the big priority rocks and then add in the filler gravel, there are still more rocks waiting outside the jar to be added than there is room inside. They're always going to stick out of our jars, shattering the edges of our lives, cutting us in the process.

Something has to be done. Balance has to be restored. And living a balanced life is not always easy, especially at first when we're sorting things out—but it's a lot easier than living in the chaos and constant exhaustion of unbalance.

One Handful Is Better

If we're going to tip the scales in a better direction, it's going to take a radical change of belief and practice. We need new thinking based on God's Word, not on the chorus of conflicting voices in the culture around us. With God's help, we can create a better life for ourselves. And I believe it starts with this key principle: "Better one handful with tranquility than two handfuls with toil and chasing after the wind" (Eccl. 4:6).

Think about what this means for a moment. It is better to have *less* of what doesn't matter and *more* of what does. It is better to have enough so that you can enjoy what you have than to have more and never enjoy it. Peace is better than stress. Less really is more.

Most of us think that if one of something is good, then two has to be better. We assume if one dollar is good, then two is better. If one car is good, then two cars must be better. If one child is good, then five kids must be better (well, that's what Tammy and I did, anyway). And if one wife is good, then two wives must

> It is better to have *less* of what doesn't matter and *more* of what does.

be—whoops! Maybe that's where it breaks down! Seriously, more is not necessarily better—especially when the pursuit of more consumes your entire life.

If more is not better, then what's the guiding principle to tip the scales of life in the right direction? We must believe that our lives function best in their God-given design—not culture-driven demands. Simply put, it's better to live by design and not by default. We must live on purpose with a clear sense of priorities focused around that purpose. Otherwise, our energy gets shotgunned in a lot of different directions. We end up firing a lot of shots but never hit any of our targets. Nothing gets accomplished, especially not the goals at the center of your bull's-eyes.

There's another reality we must consider in this equation of design. If we don't prioritize our lives, someone else will. If we don't discover God's design for our lives and live them on purpose, then we will be overtaken by the pulls and pushes of those around us. God alone knows how many days we have and how we should spend them. "All the days ordained for me were written in your book before one of them came to be" (Ps. 139:16). Only God has the answer, and only he can give us divine direction.

> Our lives function best in their God-given design—not culture-driven demands.

Without God, we will lose our way, chasing after things that don't really matter like a hamster on a wheel. His way is not about quantity but about quality. God's Word makes it clear that it's better to get the *right* things done, not *more* things done. "An intelligent person aims at wise action, but a fool starts off in many directions" (Prov. 17:24 GNT). Or, as I once heard someone say, "If you're burning the candle at both ends, you're not as bright as you think you are."

Remember, it's better to have only a little with peace of mind than to be busy all the time with more.

Running My Race

If trying to keep up with other people is not the solution, if going faster doesn't work, and if chasing more always fails, then how do you find your own unique balance? I'm convinced it's by discovering your life's unique pace and rhythm. If our culture stopped celebrating busyness as a measurement of self-importance, then each of us would have the freedom to run our own God-paced race. "Let us throw off everything that hinders and the sin that so easily entangles. And let us run with perseverance the race marked out for us" (Heb. 12:1).

While everyone's race pace will vary, I believe there are three practices that help us all discover what ours should be. Again, I don't have all the answers or know exactly what's needed to restore balance in your life, but God does—and here are some ways you can invite him to determine the tempo of your time here on earth.

First, *regularly take inventory.* Have you ever noticed how businesses take an annual inventory? Maybe you've even been in a store like Walmart or Target when they had all the merchandise tagged and counted across the store. They do this regularly to keep track of what they have and what they need, and it helps them determine what to do with the space allocations in each department. It's a simple but effective practice that we would do well to emulate in our lives. Otherwise, it's far too easy for the tide of culture, with all its trends, temptations, and trials, to sweep us away. We may have good intentions about correcting our course when we're diverted, but unless we check our direction regularly, we gravitate toward those other demands. Those demands may seem urgent and necessary, but often they are simply distractions that take us further off course.

One of the most helpful things I've started doing is taking inventory of my life on a weekly basis. And you can try it too. On your Sabbath—the day you rest and honor God—taking inventory can be a vital way to make sure you're putting him first. As a part of your worship, it helps you restore focus to your life and correct any unbalances before they press down too heavily and send you careening off course.

To discern what's essential, we need space to think, reflect, sleep, and decide. It's as King David prayed:

> LORD, remind me how *brief my time* on earth will be.
> Remind me that my days are *numbered*—
> how *fleeting* my life is.
> You have made my life no longer than the width of my hand.
> My entire lifetime is just a moment to you;
> at best, each of us is but a breath.
>
> (Ps. 39:4–5 NLT, emphasis mine)

Perhaps this is why the message Belshazzar received focused first on realizing his days were numbered (*mene*) and then used this truth to motivate him to look at how he spent them (*tekel*).

When we recognize the limited amount of time we have, we tend to make the most of it. Otherwise, we take it for granted and distract ourselves from the stark reality of our mortality. But like the individuals I interviewed during our 30 Days to Live campaign, when you're counting your days, you make them count.

In addition to my Sabbath inventories, another way I take inventory on a regular basis is by conducting a monthly evaluation. Once a month, I set aside a time to check myself in twelve key areas. Inspired by Wayne Cordeiro's book *Leading on Empty*, I grade myself in each of the key areas he identifies and write one sentence describing what I can do better. Mine aren't necessarily the same as yours. You may decide you have more or less than twelve, but here are mine just to inspire you as you consider your own key areas:

Honest evaluation on a regular basis is the key to a life of balance.

Faith	Social
Marriage	Attitude
Family	Finances
Work/Job	Creativity
Computer	Physical
Ministry	Travel

Next, *we must make tough decisions.* The key here is "elimi-nation." We all have things that don't need to be in our lives. If we're going to restore balance and focus on our true priorities, then we have to eliminate the nonessential. Something's got to go. I was recently reminded of this truth while reading the book *Essentialism: The Disciplined Pursuit of Less* by Greg McKeown.

Whether the author knew he was reinforcing a principle from the Bible, I don't know. But I do know that he included a crucial truth about the consequences of eliminating what we don't need: if we learn to say no, we'll trade popularity for respect.

This rings so true, especially when I consider all the tempta-tions I gave into while growing up. In fact, looking back, almost everything "bad" I did for the first time occurred while sleeping over at a friend's house. First time I drank alcohol? Sleeping over at a friend's house. First time smoking cigarettes? At a friend's house. Looking at magazines I shouldn't have seen? You guessed it, while spending the night at a friend's house! Which explains why I never let my kids spend the night away from home their entire lives!

Whether we're younger or older, we have to stop trying to do what everyone else is doing. We have to quit saying yes to those who offer us something that will take us in the wrong direction. Unless we set boundaries and say no to nonessentials, we will never be able to make our highest and best contributions to the things that matter most. "Teach us to number our days and recognize how few they are; help us to spend them as we should" (Ps. 90:12 TLB).

> If it isn't a clear yes, it's a clear no.

Don't try to fit everything into your life. And don't grapple with tradeoffs and continual compromises. If it isn't a clear yes, it's a clear no.

Remember: evaluate, eliminate, execute.

Finally, *focus on things that will last.* This is the highest level of living, the key to a balanced, productive, and fulfilling life.

As we consider the various places we spend our time and focus, we should continually ask ourselves, "Will this matter one hundred years from now?" I suspect you'll discover, as I have, that there are few things that fit this criteria. In fact, those things that will last generally come down to two categories: God and other people.

As we've discussed already, one of the best ways to practice an eternal perspective is to make sure we always place God first in our lives. God always matters. "But seek first his kingdom and his righteousness, and all these things will be given to you as well" (Matt. 6:33). All significance in our lives derives from who he is and how he's made us.

Many of us would say with our mouths that God matters, but our time, money, and affections point to other things. You might recall how Jesus told the story of a very successful guy, someone with everything on the outside but nothing much on the inside.

Filling his silos and barns mattered more to him than knowing God. Despite being warned about the power of his own greed, this man ignored caution and focused on accumulating more wealth.

> All significance in our lives derives from who he is and how he's made us.

But God said to him, "You fool! This very night your life will be demanded from you. Then who will get what you have prepared for yourself?"

This is how it will be with whoever stores up things for themselves but is not rich toward God. (Luke 12:20–21)

How will the scales tip when the balance of your days is measured on God's scale? At that final weighing, I suspect we will all understand what Paul wrote:

But whatever were gains to me I now consider loss for the sake of Christ. What is more, I consider everything a loss because of the surpassing worth of knowing Christ Jesus my Lord, for whose sake I have lost all things. I consider them garbage, that I may gain Christ. (Phil. 3:7–8)

It all comes down to this: our treasure is in heaven, so everything we do or choose should be about getting ready for heaven, for spending eternity with God, and helping others get there too.

At our church, we believe that real life change, the result of a shift toward an eternal perspective, happens in the context of our small groups. In other words, if you really want to focus on what matters, then you must be willing to get into real relationships with others. This is how we love, serve, support, and encourage one another. We all go through seasons when we need others to lift us up, as well as times when we're privileged to walk alongside and serve those in need. "A person standing alone can be attacked and defeated, but two can stand back-to-back and conquer. Three are even better, for a triple-braided cord is not easily broken" (Eccl. 4:12 NLT).

Take a moment to consider how you are investing in your life right now. Are the right people a priority in your life? Is your focus on things that will endure for eternity?

A Still, Small Voice

With its many demands, distractions, and disruptions, our culture often sends our lives way out of balance, exerting pressure to yield to the urgency around us. We get caught up in trying to have it all and instead end up losing our focus on what matters most. Balance comes from relying on God's purpose and his timing—not the clamor and hustle of the culture around us.

Again, why does this matter so much? How does it help you live a godly life in an ungodly culture?

Because once we make our decisions about who we are in this culture and what we believe about this culture, we're to be salt and light in it. God's plan to bring light to the dark culture is us. But the truth is, we have just as many issues as those God has called us to impact.

> God's plan to bring light to the dark culture is us.

Simply put, we can't make a difference if we're not different.

If you find this chapter as convicting as I do, then I suspect God has been nudging you for longer than the last few pages. In fact, Scripture tells us how he does it:

The LORD said, "Go out and stand on the mountain in the presence of the LORD, for the LORD is about to pass by."

Then a great and powerful wind tore the mountains apart and shattered the rocks before the LORD, but the LORD was not in the wind. After the wind there was an earthquake, but the LORD was not in the earthquake. After the earthquake came a fire, but the LORD was not in the fire. And after the fire came a gentle whisper. (1 Kings 19:11–12)

Like my old friend, the bathroom scale, God is waiting on us all the time, whispering gently into our lives. Just as my scale isn't mad at me, neither is God. He's not yelling at us. He's just constantly reminding us to consider weighing our lives. If we take time to listen, he will speak into our hearts, and maybe we'll hear one of these messages:

Slow down. You're going too fast.
Don't do it. You know it will cost you dearly.
Do it. Take the step. Go all-in with God.
Hang in there. I know you're tired. But you can make it.
Let it go—forgive them. I know they were wrong. But
    it's affecting you more than it's affecting them.
Get help. You can't overcome that problem by yourself.
There's more. Keep pursuing God. Don't settle
    for what you've experienced.

Or maybe you'll hear God whisper something unique that he's never told anyone else. Either way, listen to him.

The scales are waiting.

Twelve

MY HEART IS DIVIDED

Tension is who you think you should
be. Relaxation is who you are.

—CHINESE PROVERB

Pull over—I think I'm having a heart attack!" I yelled, holding my chest as if to catch my heart when it popped out.

The driver, a friend and fellow pastor, immediately screeched to a halt on the road's shoulder and dialed 000, the Australian equivalent of 911. We were driving along Australia's Western Coast on our way to a pastors' conference. After flying for nearly thirty hours to get from my home in Birmingham, Alabama, to Sydney, and then preaching a half-dozen times in three days, I was running on fumes and Starbucks. But this was more than just jet lag—I had never experienced this kind of chest pain before.

I was trembling and felt light-headed, and I truly thought I had only minutes to live. Waiting for the ambulance to arrive, I gave this pastor final words to share with my wife and kids. The next thing I knew, I was being loaded onto a gurney by paramedics.

"Please—don't let me die!" I pleaded to them. "I just want to go home and see my family one more time."

After nine hours in the hospital, my heart finally calmed down and seemed to check out okay. The doctor, sounding very much like Bruce the Shark from *Finding Nemo*, told me it was likely a severe panic attack and that I should have further testing done as soon as possible. He wanted to keep me there for a week, but I just wanted to go home.

By the next day, I felt much better and decided to honor my commitment to speak at the pastors' conference before flying home at the end of the week. Once I got home, I had my regular doctor check me out, and he recommended a cardiac catheterization so that they could go into my heart and take pictures. If anything was wrong with my ventricles or valves, the cath would show it.

After the test, my doctor said, "Well, there's good news and bad news. The good news is that your heart is perfect."

"Thank you, Lord!" I said. "And the bad news?"

"The bad news is that you're crazy!" my doctor said, and we laughed together. He's a good friend and a member of our church, so he knew he could tease me. He went on to explain that the culprit was a perfect storm of jet lag, excess caffeine, exhaustion, dehydration, and sleep deprivation. "Your body lasted as long as it could—even after you went past your limits," the doctor explained. "But it had to send you a serious warning sign to stop, rest, and restore your body before it was too late. You have to slow down."

I took his warning—and my body's—seriously and made many immediate, long-term adjustments to my lifestyle. Now, in addition to keeping ample margins around events requiring travel, I rest more and am conscious of pacing myself. I also drink much less caffeine, especially when I'm tired. I've made these changes, not only to avoid a scare like that again, but also because I have things I know God wants me to do yet. My Aussie breakdown forced me to stop and ask myself, "If my life is falling apart, how can I be a part of God's plan to help others?"

Perhaps the greatest symptom of our shifting culture is

ongoing, escalating, life-draining stress. We're busy and always behind, racing to catch up and get ahead, but we're never quite arriving. Our stress distracts us from realizing that our days are slipping through our fingers without enough focus on what should be our true priority: making a difference in our culture.

I fear many times we try to change the symptoms of our stress rather than the actual cause—a divided heart. We think if we only manage our time differently, or use a different scheduling system, or become a better multitasker (finally), then we'll experience less stress. But this is rarely the case! From my experience, these attempts give me an initial false illusion that I have things under control, which means I take on more responsibilities than I would've otherwise. For me, trying to address these peripheral areas without seeing the main problem only creates more stress.

To get to the heart of the issue (sorry, I couldn't resist), we must look inside ourselves and see what our primary focus is each day. We all know in theory that we want to put God first, but practicing it as a lifestyle becomes challenging in a culture that doesn't place value on God or his ways. To become wholehearted in our devotion to God, we have to make sure we're grounded and growing in our relationship with him.

God's hope is for us to meet him and know him and love him. This way our relationship with him becomes the motivation for all that we do. He wants to minister to our needs and brokenness so that we can discover our place in this world and make a difference. But when we get caught up in our own busyness, like I did in Australia, our hearts become divided between what the world tells us is important to be spending our time on (work above all else, achievements, busyness, self-gratification, and on and on) and what is truly important—our relationship with God. If we want to stand strong in a bow-down culture, we must focus singularly on God and our relationship with him, out of which will flow both a healthier daily life and a more rightly aligned heart of service.

Divided in the Danger Zone

You'll recall how the "handwriting's on the wall" has become a colloquial phrase meaning "a sense of impending doom." This same prophetic warning applies to us today—our stress is just a symptom of the spiritual disease threatening to consume us. God in his goodness always tries to warn us. For King Belshazzar, the final word in his message from God, as translated by Daniel, was *parsin*, which literally means "divided."

Like the preceding parts of this prophetic message, this warning cautions us about the consequences of living our lives divided. Just as my stressed-out body sent me a message that it could not continue functioning the way things were, God cautions us against dividing ourselves into fragments— our health, our relationships, our potential, everything in our lives. If we don't change, this division and fragmentation will destroy us.

> Our stress is just a symptom of the spiritual disease threatening to consume us.

So how do we keep it from happening? The first step is simply to pay attention to the warning signs. For too long, I had ignored my body's signals—fatigue, weariness, jittery feelings, accelerated heart rate—and just pushed through. When I didn't heed my body's warning, it kept repeating the message louder and louder until I couldn't ignore it any longer.

Similarly, God will always try to get our attention first. He knows that we need reminders about what's best for us instead of relying on what we want to do or think is best for us. God's laws and principles are always for our protection, health, and well-being—not to limit us, inhibit our freedom, or force our obedience. Warning signs, like the yellow caution light blinking beside the road, caution us to slow down and pay attention. God wants us to recognize what needs to be done and do it instead of continuing to force our own agenda.

If you're alive and functioning at even a minimal level in our world today, then you've likely experienced these warnings. You feel it in your body, your soul, your mind—a weariness that resembles burnout. There's too much information, too much to be done, and never enough time to do even half of it. You feel it in your marriage and in your family as your competing schedules pull you in all different directions.

> God's laws and principles are always for our protection, health, and well-being—not to limit us, inhibit our freedom, or force our obedience.

No one wants to self-destruct, but if you don't heed the messages you've been receiving, then you will.

Here are four warning signs that tell you perhaps it's time to make some dramatic changes in your life. If you identify with any one of these, let alone more than one, then you're in a danger zone.

First, *sin seems more attractive than usual.* When we're physically tired and mentally fatigued, our resistance is lowered. Our normal defenses and daily disciplines crumble as we succumb to exhaustion and weariness. This is when our Enemy often intensifies his attacks. This is when the risk of sinful choices increases. We're told, "Be careful, or your hearts will be weighed down with carousing, drunkenness and the anxieties of life, and that day will close on you suddenly like a trap" (Luke 21:34).

Second, *your emotions are inconsistent.* We all have attitude issues from time to time. We all struggle through the occasional bad day when nothing seems to go right. But have you ever been going through a day while feeling like you're fighting to keep a lid on your emotions? When our minds are racing and life feels overwhelming, our emotions tend to pinball around inside us. We think, *Where did that come from?* or wonder, *Why am I so short-fused right now?* The answer is simple: it's a warning sign.

When we get in a hurry, our tempers speed up too. When we're running late, it's natural to feel like yelling at other drivers on the highway. When work becomes overwhelming, it's easier to snap at coworkers. When relationships get strained at home, we're prone to argue more. Basically, we allow our circumstances to control our emotions and rob us of the joy and peace God wants us to have.

Sometimes we're running so fast we fail to stop and enjoy the touch of our spouses, the taste of a meal, or the warm feeling of sunshine on our skin. We become so jumpy that we miss the joy. I challenge you to answer this question as honestly as possible: When's the last time you really experienced joy?

If it's been longer than a week, or if you can't remember the last time your heart felt light, then consider it a warning light on your soul's dashboard.

Third, *you have become less productive.* Scripture says, "A person in a hurry makes mistakes" (Prov. 19:2 GW). It's true: the faster you go, the less you'll produce. Why? Because we fail to practice the principle that Stephen Covey calls "sharpening the saw." We forget that we can get more done if we stop once in a while and sharpen ourselves and hone our

> The faster you go, the less you'll produce.

abilities. "Careful planning puts you ahead in the long run; hurry and scurry puts you further behind" (Prov. 21:5 MSG).

Last, *you can't hear God.* So often people ask me why God

isn't speaking to them, usually about some matter they continue to bring before him in prayer. But whenever I begin to ask them about their prayer lives, it becomes clear that there are too many competing voices in their lives. God is still speaking, but they can't hear him because the ambient noise of life is just too loud.

I suspect this explains why the Bible tells us, "Be still, and know that I am God" (Ps. 46:10). Consider that a moment.

Be.

Still.

When was the last time you stopped long enough for God to speak?

How often do you quiet your soul before him?

From Hectic to Holy

Once you begin to hear God's voice and heed his warnings, what should you do? The personal changes you need to make will vary from person to person. If you listen to his whispers, the Holy Spirit will guide you and reveal what you need to stop doing and what you should start doing. In the midst of this personalized plan, however, there are some clear principles that apply to all of us, all the time.

Perhaps no principle is greater than the one God gave thirty-five hundred years ago: to keep the Sabbath Day holy. The word *Sabbath* means a day of rest, a day set aside to stop, listen, review, rest, and re-create. God knew that our bodies, minds, and spirits need such rest for replenishment. After all, he himself rested on the seventh day of creation, we're told (see Gen. 2:2). God knows we can get more done in six days than we can in seven. It's like the principle of the tithe; we can get more out of the 90 percent than the 100 percent.

The Sabbath declares that we cannot do life without God and

reminds us of our dependence on him. When we get busy, it's easy to become self-absorbed and self-important, thinking we're somebody special. We conquer and create all week long, which often inflates our sense of self-importance. Practicing the Sabbath once a week keeps us focused and prioritized regarding our place within God's plan. The Sabbath keeps us humble and holy, set apart.

God instituted this law to keep the Sabbath Day holy when he freed the Israelites from slavery (Ex. 20:8–10). They had known only slavery for generations in Egypt—they were owned, mere possessions of the world around them. But God didn't want his people owned by the world. He wanted his people to stand apart from the world and its ways.

> Practicing the Sabbath once a week keeps us focused and prioritized regarding our place within God's plan.

Accordingly, the Sabbath is a day to celebrate our freedom from human rule and human oppression. As God's children, we are free to live out our real purpose, to serve our Lord—not the competing agendas of those around us. We don't have to be swept away by the demanding and ever-changing winds of our culture's expectations.

For one day a week, the Sabbath is a regular reminder that our help comes from God. He is our strength. When we violate the Sabbath and treat it as any other day, we're saying our work is equal to God's. However, when we honor it, it restores our perspective and contrasts our humanity with God's holiness.

Sometimes people ask whether keeping the Sabbath is still valid because it comes from Old Testament Law. Yes! The first half of the Bible is just as valuable as the second half. And when I answer, I usually point out something from the New Testament:

"There remains, then, a Sabbath-rest for the people of God; for anyone who enters God's rest also rests from their works, just as God did from his. Let us, therefore, make every effort to enter that rest" (Heb. 4:9–11). Seems clear, doesn't it?

If you haven't been keeping the Sabbath, it may feel like it takes a lot of work just to rest at first. You have to relearn how to stop, to relax, to unplug from all the phones, tablets, laptops, and devices in your life. You realize the importance of intentional living as you begin to reorder your life. You learn how to rest again.

Remember the Sabbath

Now that we know the significance of keeping the Sabbath, how do we go about doing it? We focus our Sabbath rest in three areas: resting our bodies, replenishing our souls, and refocusing our spirits.

Let's begin with your body. Just as my panic attack in Australia reminded me of my body's fundamental need for rest, you probably have had your own similar experience. You may even be at the end of your rope right now, exhausted, overwhelmed, on a depressing treadmill of what feels like never-ending, life-draining busyness. You know you need rest, but you're not willing to stop and make it the priority it has to be.

You see, rest is not just sleep. Rest is a change of pace, a slower tempo, coming to a complete stop and allowing yourself to unclench, unwind, and unleash all the tension you've been carrying. Virtually every medical study, clinical trial, and doctor's experience reinforces our bodies' need for rest. When our bodies rest, healing takes place, new cells are generated, and muscles release their tautness from so much use. Rest is essential.

Keeping your Sabbath should also include a deliberate emphasis on replenishing your soul. By soul, I mean your mind, your psyche, and your emotions. Our souls get so depleted by all the harried rushing around and hurrying up. We need quietness. We need space to bring our thoughts and feelings back to a place of equilibrium. Like streams depleted of their water, our souls need time to allow the underground springs of God's refreshment to bubble up and refill their emptiness.

One of the most ancient disciplines of spiritual practice is solitude. In solitude we experience quietness and empty our minds of the jumbled thoughts and tangled emotions we've been carrying around. Instead of the constant activity we're used to, quiet solitude allows us to regain our perspective, reaffirm our priorities, and reconnect with God. The psalmist David, a former shepherd boy, knew this need: "He makes me lie down in green pastures, he leads me beside quiet waters, he refreshes my soul" (Ps. 23:2–3). If we're not careful, if we don't practice solitude, then God will force us to lie down. It's much better if we intentionally give our souls time to replenish.

> Real rest doesn't come from simply resting; it comes when your soul is connected to God's power.

In addition to solitude, our souls find replenishment through activities that nourish them and feed our imaginations. Remember that recreation—a term used to describe our hobbies and pleasurable pursuits—comes from re-creation. In other words, we need to play! When we play, our souls experience the fun of being unleashed from the constant demands to produce, to rush, to focus. "A cheerful heart is good medicine, but a crushed spirit dries up the bones" (Prov. 17:22).

We also replenish our souls through fellowship with other people. When was the last time you enjoyed a relaxed, not-looking-at-the-clock conversation with a friend or loved one? Maybe over a cup of coffee or a leisurely meal? One of the reasons that Italy is my favorite place in the world to visit is because of the relaxed, sacred respect they have for food and for meals. They invest time in preparing delicious dishes and then serve them over numerous courses, usually taking three or four hours. For me, pasta definitely replenishes my soul! And remember: *stressed* spelled backward is *desserts*. I'm just saying!

Finally, keeping your Sabbath must include allowing time for your spirit to refocus. Ultimately, real rest doesn't come from simply resting; it comes when your soul is connected to God's power. Personal renewal comes from trusting him with your worries, cares, and burdens. The heart of keeping the Sabbath is spending time—relaxed, intimate, restful time—with God.

True Sabbath is about acknowledging God and worshipping him as your Creator, Lord, and Savior. This kind of connection to God refocuses your spirit on the things that matter most. We recenter our lives on God as our life source.

And that's what Sabbath is all about.

Intentional Grounding

I've been a follower of Jesus for a long time, and I have been in ministry for more than thirty years. All this really means is that I've learned a lot of lessons and picked up on some patterns in my life and the lives of others. And for the record, let me say that experience isn't the best teacher—*evaluated* experience is how we learn and grow wiser.

Considering that, here's what I've learned over my years in ministry about remaining whole and wholehearted. First, I'm not tempted the same way every day. Without a doubt, temptations rise when I'm tired. By the end of a weekend of preaching, I'm wiped out. After spending all week preparing and praying, I give my all and have nothing left—including my usual defenses. With my energy low and my defenses down, the Enemy strikes; it's just the opportunity he's been waiting for. He's always looking for an opportune time to hit your weak spots.

To combat these attacks, I look to Jesus. When he was tempted in the wilderness, Jesus overcame the Devil with the Word of God. We're told, "When the devil had finished all this tempting, he left him until an opportune time" (Luke 4:13). For me, I make sure I know myself well enough to prepare in advance for these times— the ones my Enemy considers "opportune"—so that I can protect myself by relying on God.

Since the scare in Australia, I've made many major changes in my lifestyle habits. It wasn't just my travel that changed; I needed to change my everyday life. So now I intentionally slow down and take Mondays off. It is my Sabbath. It's the way I stay grounded in my life and in my relationships.

I get accountability from others by sharing my vulnerabilities and asking for their help. I've talked with Tammy about how vulnerable I feel during those times when I'm depleted from all the work of the week. We are very intentional about our closeness during that time; it's often when we enjoy our date for that week by having a special lunch or dinner together. She has become my protective ally.

I'm convinced that the only way to really make it in today's culture is to be intentional. This means listening to the warning signs, having a pace that's healthy and sustainable, and making my relationship with God my first priority, always. I don't want to start well but not finish the race.

How about you? What warning signs are trying to get your attention right now? What changes do you need to make? The only way to live a godly life in an ungodly culture is by remembering that your days are numbered, your life will be weighed, and your heart will be distracted and divided. Putting God first enables you to make the most of your time here on earth, to keep your life balanced by your divine purpose, and to protect your whole heart.

Don't wait until you have a breakdown.

Do it *now*.

Part 5

Culture's Greatest Need: Truth and Grace

How Do I Connect with Others?

Thirteen

CONNECTING BEFORE CORRECTING

You cannot antagonize and influence at the same time.

—J. S. KNOX

It was Friday afternoon, and I was flying from Birmingham to Boston to preach that night at a friend's church. It had been a long week, and I was making a mad dash to get to the airport. After connecting through Cincinnati, I boarded the last leg of my journey knowing exactly what I wanted to do during the flight: take a nap. I was tired and knew a little nap would allow me to recharge and do my best in delivering that night's sermon. I found my window seat, got settled, claimed my half of the armrest, and nestled against the window, shutting my eyes. I didn't want to talk; I didn't want to have to be friendly and chatty; I just wanted to catch some winks.

Next thing I knew, my seatmate arrived, tossing his newspaper beside me as he proceeded to shove his carry-on into the bin. Now, I have to confess: I was still pretending to be asleep. This guy just looked like a talker, if you know what I mean. He plopped into his seat and immediately took off his jacket, hitting me with his sleeve in the process. Not only that, but he elbowed me off the armrest! No apology, no "Oh, sorry!"—nothing.

Nonetheless, as our plane took off, I thought I was home free. That is, until he elbowed me in the ribs. Finally opening my eyes,

I looked over at him, about ready to let him have it, when he asked, "So, what kind of work do you do?"

I sighed and watched my nap evaporate. It was going to be a long flight.

For Crying Out Loud

Okay, another confession: this question always sparks a dilemma for me. One way or another, people always react when you tell them you're a pastor. They either want to debate you on some issue, or they want pastoral counseling about a burden they're carrying. It's not that I'm not happy to tell people I'm a pastor . . . it's just that sometimes, well, I'd rather take a nap.

But I sensed my nap was not going to happen, so I went ahead and told the truth. Immediately, this middle-aged man began losing it—deep, guttural, belly sobbing. It was loud and messy; everyone on our plane knew the guy in 23B was crying.

I gave him a moment to try and collect himself and then asked his name.

"Billy," he said in between sniffles.

"What's wrong, Billy? Why are you so upset, my friend?" I said.

He shook his head as another wave of tears flooded his cheeks. "I . . . just . . . buried . . . my best friend . . . back in Cincinnati. Had a massive heart attack when he picked up his little girl. Now . . . I'm never . . . going to see him . . . again!" By this time, Billy had the hiccups as well.

I immediately thought of this verse in 1 Thessalonians and shared it with him: "Brothers and sisters, we do not want you to be uninformed about those who sleep in death, so that you do not grieve like the rest of mankind, who have no hope" (4:13).

"No, don't start that Bible stuff on me," Billy said adamantly before adding, "I'm Jewish."

"Well, Jesus was Jewish," I said.

"Really? Okay, go on then," he said.

Seriously, I couldn't make this stuff up! That's what he said. After I repeated the verse and explained what it meant, Billy said, "How do I get that kind of hope?" He teed up my opportunity to share the gospel with him, so that's exactly what I did. By the time we landed, Billy and I had talked more about what it means to follow Jesus, how religion has messed up what it means to be a Christian, and how God loves and forgives us. I was a little disappointed as we walked off the plane together that we didn't have more time. Billy was so close to the threshold of salvation.

"God bless you, Billy," I said, extending my hand to shake his. "Here's my card if you want to talk some more."

"No, no," he said and stopped there in the terminal. "We have to finish this right now. Tell me how I can give my life to Jesus."

As I began to pray, Billy grabbed my hands and we stood there in the Boston airport. He prayed after me and became a Christian. I'll never forget that experience for lots of reasons, but mostly because it taught me two important lessons. First, this life is not about me—my priority of napping couldn't compare to what Billy needed. He was hurting and had just lost his best friend. He didn't need anyone arguing theology with him or comparing Judaism to Christianity. He needed an ear, someone willing to listen and care about him and his grief.

> People are ready for God, but they want hope, not a debate.

Second, I was reminded that my purpose as a follower of Jesus is to give people hope. People are ready for God, but they want hope, not a debate. This is where we have an opportunity. I know that many of us find it difficult and sometimes painfully awkward to engage others on this level and share the gospel—there was a time when I felt this way too—but if what people are really looking for in the end is hope, not a high-level intellectual debate, we are already equipped to meet them in that need!

As followers of Jesus, we have real hope.

And we're called to share it.

But *how* we share it makes a difference.

Looking for the One

Relating and connecting with people before we tell them about God precedes the early church and followers of Jesus sharing the gospel. During his seventy-year captivity, Daniel also shared his faith with each king of Babylon who ruled during that time. Instead of separating himself from his culture, he made an impact on it without compromising his beliefs. Through four different regimes, he gained influence and pointed people to God.

How did Daniel do this? He didn't do it by coercion but by persuasion. The exceptional qualities and godly character Daniel displayed attracted his captors and commanded their respect. Daniel knew what we must remember in our interactions with others today: connect before we correct. Reaching people is our purpose.

While we don't have record of the conversations between Daniel and each of the four Babylonian kings under whom he served, we can tell that Daniel was obviously doing something right. His responses must have reflected respect, humility, and diplomacy without compromise. Daniel didn't argue, explain, criticize, or condemn the Babylonian leaders—even though he sometimes had a right to do so. Remember when the jealous satraps manipulated King Darius and had Daniel thrown into the lions' den (see Dan. 6)?

As we noted before in this story, Darius was obviously fond of Daniel and respected his Jewish prisoner enough to promote Daniel to a position of leadership. Just consider how remarkable this appointment was. The Babylonians seized an entire nation of the Jewish people, but one of them so impressed them for not assimilating and conforming to their culture that they made him a leader in their government. From this, I infer that Darius not only respected Daniel but he trusted Daniel as well. Most leaders would likely worry about Daniel being a spy or trying to free his people. But apparently Daniel's sincerity and authenticity erased any doubts in the king's mind.

> Connect before we correct. Reaching people is our purpose.

Daniel knew that the way he represented God mattered. He understood that his character, attitude, and demeanor mattered just as much as his words and actions. Daniel became a person of influence in the pagan culture of Babylon because he maintained his convictions and exercised his faith in a manner that reflected honesty, openness, and curiosity. We can learn so much from his example.

Before Christ, our entire lives are about finding God and letting God do a work in us. But once that happens, our mission on earth changes. Just like Daniel in the decadent, sinful, anything-goes world of Babylon, this is our purpose in our generation—to influence it for Christ.

Maybe you're thinking, *Well, Chris, I'm just not really comfortable sharing my faith—you know, talking about something so personal. I don't want to cram my beliefs down anyone's throat. It's easy for you to share your faith—you're a pastor. And Daniel was, well, Daniel! I'm just shy when it comes to talking about God with other people.* Fair enough. I know it's not always easy and that sometimes you don't know what to say. But that's okay—it's really not as hard as you might think. Sharing your faith is all about relationship, not right answers or slick presentations.

> Sharing your faith is all about relationship, not right answers or slick presentations.

It's undeniably clear in Scripture that Jesus commanded all his followers, not just those in full-time ministry, to share the good news with everyone around them. "Jesus said to his followers, 'Go everywhere in the world, and tell the Good News to everyone'" (Mark 16:15 NCV). You don't have to be well spoken or have a dramatic story to tell; you just have to be real. Paul wrote, "We are Christ's ambassadors; God is making his appeal through us" (2 Cor. 5:20 NLT).

But it's become difficult in an increasingly skeptical world. Unfortunately, some Christians think their purpose is to argue. They feel compelled to get in people's faces, tell them what they're doing wrong, and demand that they change. The way they share their faith—if we can even call it that—is dogmatic, angry, and downright offensive. No wonder it turns people off; it turns me off! And I suspect it turns God off.

Why do I think this? Because Jesus told us he is the Good Shepherd, willing to leave the ninety-nine sheep to seek out the one that's lost. Our motive for sharing our faith must always be grounded in this kind of urgent, loving attitude.

The kind a parent has for a lost child.

Finding Joseph

"Where's Joseph? I don't see him," my wife said. *"We've lost Joseph!"*

A jolt of panic surged through me. Our autistic son, only twelve years old, was missing.

It happened so quickly. Our family was vacationing with two other families, and it was the very last day of our trip. We'd gone into a coffee shop and decided to head over to the ice cream parlor next door. All twenty of us had made the transition next door—except our son Joseph. We didn't realize he'd gone to the bathroom, and he never saw us walk next door. When he came out and we weren't there, he exited the coffee shop and went searching for us in the opposite direction. By the time we realized he wasn't with us, he was nowhere in sight.

Because of his inability to communicate and other unique challenges, Joseph was in extreme danger off on his own. My mind raced with terrible possibilities and worst-case scenarios. Compounding my fear was the horror of the knowledge that a child in that same area recently had been kidnapped and killed. We had to find him—fast.

We spent an excruciating twenty-five minutes frantically searching the area. Finally, I spotted him. He was crossing a footbridge, dazed by his own confused panic and blinding tears. "Joseph!" I yelled. Then I ran and embraced him. To this day, I can still close my eyes and feel him melt into me with the most extreme relief. Fear and panic dissipated into a sweaty and teary reunion. He was lost. But now he was found.

Tears mist my eyes as I type these words even now. Nothing could describe how desperate I had been for my lost son in those twenty-five minutes. I was so completely consumed with finding him that nothing else could possibly have come close to comforting me or stopping my search. Other things became completely irrelevant.

If one of my other kids had stopped me in the middle of our search for Joseph and asked me, "Hey, Dad, what's for dinner?" I would have looked at them with complete dismay. Their question on its own is not bad, but in light of their brother being missing I would probably have replied, "*Really?!* That's what you're thinking about right now? Where is your concern for your brother?"

God has this same kind of desperation for his lost kids. I can't help but wonder if he listens to some of our ponderings and questions and thinks, *In light of the fact that 4.5 billion of my children are lost, is that really what you're going to think about right now?* Granted, God is completely compassionate about all our questions, but, boy, did those twenty-five minutes without my precious son Joseph help shed some light on God's Father's heart for the lost.

God passionately and fervently asks us to go into all the world and tell his lost children about his love. But we will never be able to do this effectively if we lose our way in the process. Let's make sure we don't start arguing about what's for dinner among ourselves and lose sight of the end goal. Let's instead follow his example and go after the one lost sheep.

Serve Grace with Salt

When we take that step toward the Father's heart and pursue the lost, though, we must keep in mind that our goal is not to sound like a lawyer giving a closing argument in the courtroom. We're not trying to prove we're right; we're just trying to be effective. Genuine. Honest. Caring. We're told, "Be wise in the way you act toward outsiders; make the most of every opportunity. Let your conversation be always full of grace, seasoned with salt, so that you may know how to answer everyone" (Col. 4:5–6). Notice this doesn't tell us to have all the answers; it simply says our conversation should be full of grace and seasoned with salt. Based in God's grace and salted for flavor—that's the recipe for sharing our faith.

While we don't have to have all the answers, we should be ready to tell others about the hope we have in Christ: "Always be prepared to give an answer to everyone who asks you to give the reason for the hope that you have" (1 Peter 3:15). This doesn't mean having a prepared speech, carrying tracts in your purse, or memorizing long passages of the Bible. It simply means you remain open to opportunities to tell others about what matters most in your life. It means having "spiritual food" to share that's full of grace and seasoned with salt.

> Jesus connected with people before he corrected them.

The first step is simply to connect with people. Everyone longs to be loved unconditionally. We all crave attention and appreciate it when others show interest in us and our lives. As Christians, we don't have to become everyone's best friend, but we should show the compassion, kindness, and honesty we see modeled by Jesus. He always put the relationship first. Jesus connected with people before he corrected them.

One of my favorite examples comes from Jesus' encounter with a certain "wee little man" (come on, you remember that song from Sunday school!) named Zacchaeus. Here is how their paths crossed one day while Christ was passing through Jericho, Zacchaeus's hometown:

> Jesus entered Jericho and was passing through. A man was there by the name of Zacchaeus; he was a chief tax collector and was wealthy. He wanted to see who Jesus was, but because he was short he could not see over the crowd. So he ran ahead and climbed a sycamore-fig tree to see him, since Jesus was coming that way.
>
> When Jesus reached the spot, he looked up and said to him, "Zacchaeus, come down immediately. I must stay at your house today." So he came down at once and welcomed him gladly.

All the people saw this and began to mutter, "He has gone to be the guest of a sinner."

But Zacchaeus stood up and said to the Lord, "Look, Lord! Here and now I give half of my possessions to the poor, and if I have cheated anybody out of anything, I will pay back four times the amount."

Jesus said to him, "Today salvation has come to this house, because this man, too, is a son of Abraham. For the Son of Man came to seek and to save the lost." (Luke 19:1–10)

There's so much for us to notice in how Jesus related to this curious outsider. And that's exactly what Zacchaeus was—a man disliked by everyone in his community, someone who had gotten rich by being a tax collector, demanding the government's money but keeping plenty for himself. He would be the equivalent of a crooked, scandal-ridden politician today, a man whom everyone liked to dislike.

But, apparently, Zacchaeus had heard things about this man called Jesus. We're told the tax collector "wanted to see who Jesus was," not hear what he had to say or learn from Christ's teachings. He just wanted to catch a glimpse of this guy he'd heard about and see for himself. And Jesus knew this, of course. The Lord understood better than anyone that people don't care what you know; first, they want to know that you care. With this awareness of Zacchaeus's curiosity, Jesus invited himself to the little man's house for dinner. He wanted to do more than a quick introduction and small talk (no pun intended, honest). Jesus wanted to show Zacchaeus how much he really cared about Zacchaeus's heart, not just his height.

> People don't care what you know; first, they want to know that you care.

Walk the Talk

The next step after connecting with people is living according to what Jesus taught. People are generally not interested in having theological debates; they want to see if we really live out what we claim to believe. They want to find out if what Jesus said about his disciples was true, that they would be known because of their love. When we truly engage with other people and demonstrate the love of Jesus, we show how much we respect them, despite whatever differences might exist between us. Even if they disagree or are not ready to make a salvation decision, they will remember another person who genuinely showed interest and concern for them.

> We have to earn someone's respect before we can build a relationship. And we have to have relationship before we can have influence.

This is so important because we have to earn someone's respect before we can build a relationship. And we have to have relationship before we can have influence. I suspect it's not even what we say that they respond to at first—it's our attitude, our body language, our willingness to look them in the eye. Our willingness to care about them as a person, not just another face in line at the store or just another passenger on the bus.

Once you have established a baseline of respect and demonstrated a willingness to relate person-to-person, then you can look for an opportunity to share your story. This is the heart of sharing your faith! Evangelism is not telling others what they should do; it's telling them what happened in you. It's never "Turn or burn!" It's "Hey, guess what happened to me." Jesus commanded, "Let your light shine before others, that they may see your good deeds and glorify your Father in heaven" (Matt. 5:16). Later, as he prepared to leave earth and send the Holy Spirit to dwell in his disciples, Jesus said, "You will be my *witnesses*, telling people about me everywhere" (Acts 1:8 NLT, emphasis mine).

Jesus didn't tell us to be his judge before others, or even his jury. He told us to be witnesses, people who simply tell what they saw firsthand. Witnesses have some kind of direct experience related to what they're describing. They know, because they saw it themselves.

That's all we have to do: let others know what God has done in our lives. It could be something he did years ago or something he did that very morning. All we have to do is intentionally drop positive God-thoughts with whomever we meet. Because everyone is going through something, we can rest assured they hurt and have need of God's love.

> The goal is to persuade, not coerce.

When you're prepared and looking for them, you'll be surprised how many opportunities will open before you. Remember: the goal is to persuade, not coerce. And when we live a life that others find appealing and authentic, it's easy to do.

Plain and Simple

Finally, if we are to be salt and light, we need to invite others to a place where they can experience God for themselves. This is usually your church, but it might be a conference, Sunday school class, Bible study, or outreach event. The key is to make sure you choose a place that's receptive to newcomers who may be skeptical or have questions. A place where they will feel welcome and appreciated.

It's vital to communicate that Jesus isn't a religion; he is someone to be experienced, directly and personally. In fact, the greatest proof of Christianity is a changed life. Religious arguments make claims, but Jesus changes lives. This is why it's so important to get seekers into an environment where they can experience the presence of God for themselves.

You will never find any person mentioned in the Scriptures who had a real encounter with the living God and still questioned God or rebelled against him. Because once you experience God in his glory, you can't turn away from him or forget his touch. One of the most dramatic conversions described in the Bible is the life of Paul.

Before Paul met Jesus, he was an angry zealot named Saul out looking to stop Jesus' followers, even if that meant killing them. And then on the road to the city of Damascus one day, he met Jesus face-to-face. Saul's name was changed to Paul, and he went on to become one of the most impactful disciples of the faith. And having had that direct, personal encounter himself, Paul wanted others to also experience God in a personal relationship.

> You'll remember, friends, that when I first came to you to let you in on God's master stroke, I didn't try to impress you with polished speeches and the latest philosophy. I deliberately kept it plain and simple: first Jesus and who he is; then Jesus and what he did—Jesus crucified.
>
> I was unsure of how to go about this, and felt totally inadequate—I was scared to death, if you want the truth of it—and so nothing I said could have impressed you or anyone else. But the Message came through anyway. God's Spirit and God's power did it, which made it clear that your life of faith is a response to God's power, not to some fancy mental or emotional footwork by me or anyone else. (1 Cor. 2:1–5 MSG)

People are only skeptical about the Bible when they try to understand faith with just their minds. What is needed is a "God encounter"—a meeting with the unforgettable power, presence, and peace of God. When they experience God for themselves, they'll see him as he is. And they will be forever changed.

Four Pictures of God

Once you've established a relationship with people, you will often discover that their way of seeing God is not accurate. Based on their families growing up, negative church experiences, or hostile encounters with other people identifying themselves as Christians, people easily develop negative, inaccurate attitudes toward God. Others might base their view of God and Christians on their exposure to certain religions, particular churches, and assorted misinformation. They have not experienced a personal encounter with Christ through the Holy Spirit.

Once we begin to identify the inaccuracies in their view of God, we may be tempted to try and correct them immediately. But often the best thing we can do is truly listen and care about what they're sharing that led to their faulty view. Showing them we understand why they view God the way they do is crucial if we are to connect and build a respectful, trustworthy relationship. Once they realize we truly care about them, then we can begin restoring and correcting how they understand and see God. Even if they continue to disagree with us, they will respect us for accepting them and understanding their views. It's important to realize you can accept someone without approving of their views, lifestyle, or behavior. As a parent, I accept my children and love them unconditionally, but I do not always approve of what they say and how they act. Connecting with people, listening and understanding them, before correcting them is paramount to being a person of influence like Daniel.

I learned just how much it means for others to feel heard and understood years ago when I was a youth pastor in Colorado. I would eat lunch with teens from church in their school cafeterias. I always encouraged them to bring their friends, and I made it a point to ask these nonbelievers questions.

"I work for a church, so I'm always curious about how people view God. What do *you* think about God?" I'd ask as casually as possible. Then I'd listen carefully, asking follow-up questions and engaging with what they told me. Eventually, I tried to make it clear that I understood why they felt the way they did about God. "I'd feel that way too," I'd say, "if I had to deal with what you've experienced." I wanted them to know I viewed them as people, not projects.

Addressing the way others misperceive God isn't a new task. In fact, this was one Jesus undertook in his time on earth:

> Jesus and his disciples went on to the villages around Caesarea Philippi. On the way he asked them, "Who do people say I am?"
>
> They replied, "Some say John the Baptist; others say Elijah; and still others, one of the prophets."
>
> "But what about you?" he asked. "Who do you say I am?"
>
> Peter answered, "You are the Messiah." (Mark 8:27–29)

Within this very brief exchange, we see four perceptions about God emerge in the disciples' response to Jesus' question. Three of them were incorrect; only the last one was a true reflection of God. These four reflect our perceptions today as well. Many of the ideas people have about God are off base for one reason or another. Like Jesus, we need to ask about and understand people's ideas first to then effectively show them the truth. Referring to John the Baptist, Elijah, and other prophets made sense in the disciples' day, but what are some of the misperceptions people commonly have today?

I first heard the four word pictures below described by my friend John Maxwell, who explores them in his teachings on leadership for corporate audiences. John is not the only one to recognize and address these four views. Many seminaries and even *USA Today* have conducted interviews and public opinion polls and emerged with these same four ways of seeing God. Before we discuss the accurate view of God, let's examine each of the incorrect views.

A Locked Gate

The first mistaken view of God can be seen in the form of a "locked gate." It reflects the myth that God cannot—and presumably does not want to—be reached. So many people think God is far away, that getting to him is a long journey with a lot of hoops to jump through, and even then they may not find him. Unfortunately, some churches and religious denominations reinforce this misperception, causing others to feel like outsiders.

These groups act like there's some secret key to get into Christianity, as if they alone are the guardians of that secret key. Their religion is like some exclusive club that must always keep those "not worthy" outside the gate. Even certain doctrines they teach say that some are picked while others aren't. But this is not what the Bible says: "He doesn't play hide-and-seek with us. He's not remote; he's *near*" (Acts 17:27 THE MESSAGE).

A Pile of Luggage

The second incorrect view of God that many people have reflects the "pile of luggage" perception. It perpetuates the myth that God can't possibly want someone who has so much baggage in their lives. People caught in this misperception assume they've made too many mistakes and have done too much for God to want them. They wrongly believe God judges them based on their past. He can't possibly love them, because they don't have every-thing all together.

But what we've done in our past is no shocking secret to God. He knows and still accepts and loves us—just as we are. In fact, that's the whole reason he sent Jesus: "But God showed his great love for us by sending Christ to die for us while we were still sinners" (Rom. 5:8 NLT). He even used people with all kinds of messed-up backgrounds to help us see the truth about his heart for us. In the Bible we see God accepting men and women with more luggage than Samsonite. Abraham, Jacob, Moses, David, Ruth, Samson, Jesus' disciples, Paul—none of them had their lives together. They made mistakes, stumbled, and fumbled, and God met them and lifted them back on their feet.

An Endless Ladder

This third false view of God sees him as an "endless ladder" who requires too much from those who seek him. People in this camp assume they must change first, that they have to work for God's acceptance by proving themselves worthy or "good enough." Others with this view get frustrated, because they know they can never do enough or be good enough. Condemnation becomes their companion. But God's Word makes it clear that there's only one thing God requires from us: belief in Jesus. "Then they asked him, 'What must we do to do the works God requires?' Jesus answered, 'The work of God is this: to believe in the one he has sent'" (John 6:28–29).

A Free Gift

The only accurate view of God is the one that sees him as our Savior and his love for us as a free gift. "Thanks be to God for his indescribable gift!" (2 Cor. 9:15). This reflects who he really is. There's nothing we have to do—nothing we can do—to win his favor or earn forgiveness. We simply have to accept the gift of grace through his Son, Jesus Christ. The Bible explains, "For it is by grace you have been saved, through faith—and this is not from yourselves, it is the *gift of God*—not by works, so that no one can boast" (Eph. 2:8–9, emphasis mine). Paul also described it this way: "For the wages of sin is death, but the *gift of God* is eternal life in Christ Jesus our Lord" (Rom. 6:23, emphasis mine).

Have you ever received an undeserved gift? A time when someone surprised you with a gift for no reason at all, other than that they care about you? It's better than getting a present on your birthday or Valentine's Day, when it's expected or "obligatory." When you receive a gift for no reason, you realize how much the giver cares about you. That person was just thinking of you and decided to give you something so you'd know it.

Jesus is this gift. A gift for us to share. But we earn the right to share this gift, not by blatantly correcting others' false notions about Jesus, but by listening, understanding, and showing them who Christ really is. Yes, it's important to be aware of these inaccurate views. But only so we can demonstrate the true power of Jesus' life-changing love.

Fourteen

THE SECRET OF INFLUENCE

Preach the gospel, and if necessary use words.

—ST. FRANCIS OF ASSISI

I heard it again this past Sunday.

Standing at the edge of the stage at Church of the Highlands, watching our "church news" video play, waiting to walk on and deliver God's Word to thousands of people, I heard a voice ask, "Who do you think you are? What makes *you* think you can do *this*?"

This voice is nothing new; I hear it every Sunday. I hear it every time I step on a stage to speak in front of people. It's the little voice in my head that tries to remind me of who I was before God started working in my life. It's the voice trying to undermine what God is doing through me.

For as long as I can remember, I've had an inferiority complex. Even though I was consistently loved and affirmed by every authority figure in my life, including my parents, I've struggled to believe in myself. I suspect much of it stems from the bullying I experienced in elementary school. Then when my high school years came along, my life didn't get much better. I loved sports but didn't have the physical body to pull them off successfully. I wasn't the greatest student either. With my best efforts, I was a

B or C student. I lived in South Louisiana, which was fiftieth on just about every list, from education to economic prospects. So how could my life have any significance when I was at the bottom of the bottom?

Even after I gave my life to Christ, I didn't think I would be very successful. I assumed, "I am who I am, and I can't change that." I was just grateful God loved me enough to save me.

As I got closer to the Lord and let his Word work in my life, something began to happen. God began to develop me into another person, one that at times I don't even recognize today. That shy, bullied, insecure little boy from South Louisiana now influences a lot of people around the world. Sometimes it's hard to believe. I'm living proof God transforms us into a brand-new people, those who grow into the fullness of who God made us to be.

Sometimes those who consider themselves the "least likely to succeed" become the most likely to touch the world around them. People tell me, "I want to be salt and light, but I just don't know what to say or how to be. I just don't think I'm cut out to share my faith the way you're talking about." That's why I like telling people about that little voice I hear, the one that tries to make me doubt what I'm capable of doing. After three decades of ministry, it's still there. But the voice of God has been, and always will be, stronger, and I hold on to the fact that "I can do all things through Christ who strengthens me" (Phil. 4:13 NKJV).

> Sometimes those who consider themselves the "least likely to succeed" become the most likely to touch the world around them.

Distinguishing Yourself

In the world we live in today, with so much moral compromise and acerbic back-and-forth between people on various sides of the issues at hand, the only hope for culture to improve is a spiritual revolution, one led by strong, loving, confident Christians. The kind of followers of Jesus who enter into culture and engage with everyone around them like a breath of fresh air. People who aren't perfect and don't claim to be, just men and women, boys and girls, trying to love God with their whole hearts, minds, and lives.

People like you and me.

This is what I love about Daniel. Most likely, he never imagined himself as a prisoner of war, someone whose strong faith not only withstood the enormous cultural pressures around him but also impressed those holding him captive. Can you imagine the pain of being taken into slavery and transported into a completely different culture? Can you imagine how it felt to be separated from family, friends, and home? Can you imagine how insecure he must have felt to live in a culture that mocked his religion and despised his lifestyle?

Yet Daniel was a man of influence, a counterculture conduit of God in an ungodly world. How did he do it? With all that going against him, how did he become someone who would influence four administrations of government in a pagan culture?

Simple. He let God transform him into the person God had always intended him to be. And if we'll live in the same space of surrender, God will also transform us into his likeness for the purpose of influencing the culture around us. By my definition, this is what true leadership is all about: influencing the culture around you. It's not surprising, then, that my favorite passage from the book of Daniel also includes my favorite verse on leadership:

It pleased Darius to appoint 120 satraps to rule throughout the kingdom, with three administrators over them, one of whom was Daniel. The satraps were made accountable to them so that the king might not suffer loss. Now Daniel so distinguished himself among the administrators and the satraps by his exceptional qualities that the king planned to set him over the whole kingdom. (Dan. 6:1–3)

Notice it doesn't say Daniel was naturally distinguished, unique, or special. I'm not very distinguished either! But the Bible says he "distinguished himself"—with exceptional qualities that impressed the king and the king's leaders. Being distinguished often comes from someone's appearance, natural ability, or quirky personality while distinguishing oneself typically relies more on what you do and how you do it. The difference is important, because it means that we can also distinguish ourselves through our attitudes, words, and behavior. We don't have to be a super saint or perfect Christian. These "exceptional qualities" were nothing special or unusual to Daniel; they all emerged on display because he simply followed God and remained firm in his faith. And, as a result, the king gave Daniel even more influence!

Daniel became an individual of note to others as he let God work in his life. The Bible talks about this kind of transformation:

Now the Lord is the Spirit, and where the Spirit of the Lord is, there is freedom. And we all, who with unveiled faces contemplate the Lord's glory, are being transformed into his image with ever-increasing glory, which comes from the Lord, who is the Spirit. (2 Cor. 3:17–18)

I love this description of the process! The Lord is the Spirit, and the word translated as *Spirit* here literally means "fresh air." In other words, the Lord brings life to our lives by giving us freedom and hope. Just as God first breathed life into Adam, our Father continues to infuse our lives with the breath of his Spirit.

God's fresh, life-giving power enables us to change. Into what? His likeness. And then we bring that freshness, that new life, everywhere we go. As others around us notice and are influenced by our words and actions, then the culture around us experiences that same transformation. Simply put, if we let God change us, it's not only good for us but for the world around us.

The Full Weight of Glory

Our present culture desperately needs this—more encounters with life-giving, fresh-air-bringing followers of Jesus. With so much turmoil in our world today, more and more people are looking for hope. The more we look and act like Jesus, the more others will find hope in God. This is how we reflect God's glory—by looking like Jesus.

So what does Jesus look like? What does "looking like Jesus" mean on a practical, day-in day-out basis? We know the earthly Jesus looked like a man, a Jewish man of ancient times during the Roman Empire. We've all seen various depictions of him in paintings and pictures, movies, and TV shows. Obviously, we're not all able to resemble him physically. Instead,

> If we let God change us, it's not only good for us but for the world around us.

we are to look like his glory. The biblical word we translate as *glory* literally means "full weight." We are to represent the "full weight" of Christ's presence to everyone around us. How do we do this? While we can answer this question in many ways, I believe a concise set of qualities emerges from this description in John's prophetic vision:

In the center, around the throne, were four living creatures, and they were covered with eyes, in front and in back. The first living creature was like a lion, the second was like an ox, the third had a face like a man, the fourth was like a flying eagle. (Rev. 4:6–7)

We see this same scene in the Old Testament. The prophet Ezekiel saw the face of God and said, "Their faces looked like this: Each of the four had the face of a human being, and on the right side each had the face of a lion, and on the left the face of an ox; each also had the face of an eagle" (Ezek. 1:10). He went on to conclude, "This was the appearance of the likeness of the glory of the LORD" (Ezek. 1:28). These four faces, these four different facets of Jesus' character, provide a symbolic, focused way for us to think about how we can be more like Jesus and share his love with our culture.

And when we do, we can have the same influence Daniel had on those around him.

Love God

As king of the jungle, the lion came to symbolize power and royal authority throughout much of history. We see lions representing royalty on various coats of arms, on shields and palaces, and in royal crests and medals. As followers of Jesus, however, our power doesn't come from a title or position of authority but from cultivating our relationship with God, the ultimate authority. And when we spend time with God, the result is boldness. "The righteous are as bold as a lion" (Prov. 28:1).

This quality of boldness, represented by the face of the lion, is on vivid display throughout the Gospel of John as he emphasizes Jesus' power as the Son of God. Scholars believe John wrote his gospel at the end of his life, around AD 90. He wrote his account of Jesus' life to demonstrate that Jesus is not just fully man but also fully God. His gospel is directed to "all who believe" and contains more about the final week of Jesus' earthly life than any other gospel. John described Christ in all his power and glory, the King of kings, the Lion of Judah.

In John's gospel, we also see how we have access to Christ's power as we grow deeper in love with Jesus. John himself is frequently referred to as the "disciple whom Jesus loved" (John 21:7). He spent time with Jesus and became devoted to sharing the good news for the rest of his life, long after Jesus' resurrection and ascension. The boldness and the courage he had to live in this way was not necessarily natural to him as a person, but it was a natural outflow of his relationship with Jesus, a reflection of the one with whom he spent so much time. In fact, the book of Acts tells us that "when they saw the courage of Peter and John and realized that they were unschooled, ordinary men, they were astonished and they took note that these men had been with Jesus" (Acts 4:13).

> The more time we spend with him, the more others can see him through our words and actions.

John's gospel, along with the face of the lion, reminds us of the importance of cultivating our relationship with God. Everything flows out of that relationship and how we spend quality time in his presence. We develop closeness with God by praying and fasting, studying his Word, and worshipping him. As a result, we develop a character that reflects God and his glory. The more time we spend with him, the more others can see him through our words and actions.

Let's take a moment for a quick, honest inventory: How much time are you spending with God on a daily basis? Are you committed to boldly being an image of God to the world? How does this commitment come out in your daily life? What needs to change?

We can't make a difference if we're not different.

Love People

The second face of Jesus, that of a man, emerges thematically throughout the Gospel of Luke. His depiction of Christ, up close and personal, focuses on Jesus as the "Son of Man" and begins by tracing Jesus' genealogy all the way back to Adam, the ideal man. Throughout Luke's writings, we find an emphasis on the way Jesus wasn't lofty, placing himself above others, but served everyone around him.

As a medical doctor by profession, Luke often includes precise medical terminology in his account of how Jesus healed the sick and infirm. Luke primarily wrote for an audience of cultured, educated Greeks and gives us the most complete, orderly, and classical description of Christ's time on earth. Luke also gives the best description of Jesus' birth and childhood and records unique stories and parables not found in the other gospels.

Throughout Luke's account, the focus remains on Jesus' ministry to people and the way it was always primarily about those people around him. Christ was attuned to people and frequently cut through everything else to address both their deepest physical and spiritual needs. If we want to be like Jesus and make a difference in our culture, then we must learn how to be people persons.

But, Chris, you might be thinking, *I'm not a people person! I'm too shy, too quiet, too embarrassed to talk about spiritual matters with others. And I don't want to make things awkward by asking about their needs. . . . This just isn't my thing.* But I disagree. We all relate to other people uniquely, but we are all called to relate, to care, to notice the people around us. Jesus talked about a lot of things, but more than any other subject he talked about relationships.

Whether healing the sick, feeding the multitudes, or washing his disciples' feet, Jesus demonstrated his greatness by putting others before himself. He lived to be a servant to all. With him as our example, we must be team players, believing we are better together. We can't go it alone. We need other people, and they need us. We must defend, protect, and encourage one another.

Practically speaking, this means we have to cultivate respect and honor the trust we build with others. We must humble ourselves just as Jesus did and remove barriers of race, gender, age, and ethnicity. In Jesus' eyes, there are no outsiders. There's no room for an attitude of "us versus them." We are all created in the image of

> In Jesus' eyes, there are no outsiders. . . . God doesn't play favorites, and neither should we.

God, and he is committed to pursuing and loving each of us so that we might know him. God doesn't play favorites, and neither should we.

Excellence

What comes to mind when you consider an eagle? Many people tend to think of a majestic bird that soars to great heights with a fierce kind of grace. This view has been established historically because the eagle has been used as a symbol of royalty and power even before the time of Christ, appearing on armor, coins, flags, and other forms of heraldry. Throughout Scripture we see only positive references to the eagle, including Psalm 103:5, Exodus 19:4, and Isaiah 40:31.

Today, of course, most of us think of the eagle as a symbol of our country, a proud emblem of our United States of America that appears on our currency, government buildings, and presidential seal. From ancient times and still today, the eagle remains a noble reminder to seek higher goals, to pursue excellence in all that we do.

It's no coincidence, then, that Matthew's gospel, traditionally symbolized by the face of the eagle, spotlights "Jesus as Messiah." We get a double dose of inspirational excellence in action here, both in Matthew's style as well as his focus. Before becoming one of Jesus' disciples, Matthew was a money guy, an accountant and tax collector accustomed to focusing on the details down to the last penny. We see his attention for detail and pursuit of excellence in the way he cites the Old Testament more than any of the other gospels. Writing the longest of the four gospels, Matthew developed his own complete bibliography to support and cross-reference various aspects of Jesus' life. Virtually every English teacher would be forced to give Matthew an A+ for his work.

Matthew not only displays excellence in his account of Jesus' life; he also focuses on Jesus as the Messiah, the Promised One whom the Jewish people had been anticipating for hundreds of years. With a lineage that descended from King David, Jesus was a king by birth. However, for the Jewish people to accept Jesus as the Messiah, most of them would want historical evidence. This is where Matthew's attention to detail shows the great pains he took to lay out the proof of Jesus' identity as the long-promised Son of God. Consequently, Matthew quoted the Old Testament prophecies extensively. He wanted to make his case clear and logical, to use familiar and historical passages that would compel his audience to consider his point seriously. Matthew wanted to do everything in his power to make sure he presented the strongest case possible.

Therefore, this third facet of who Jesus is directs us, his image-bearers, toward a commitment to excellence. We are to live respectable lives and let all that we do be done to the best of our ability. We place a huge value on this truth at Church of the Highlands. We want everything we do to reflect excellence—not back at us and our efforts, but to our Source. Attention to excellence in how we create an environment for people to experience God attracts people and allows them to relax and be comfortable. They feel respected and appreciated by the care we take on their behalf. Being comfortable allows people to be receptive.

If we want to stand out like Daniel, then we need to display a willingness to do our best at all times. In addition to such attention to detail, we need to do it in ways that don't garner praise for ourselves but for God. No one is perfect and we don't want to get hung up on our own, or someone else's, expectations, but when we focus on Christ and continually point the fruit of all our efforts back at him, we can do all things well, as if we were doing them for Jesus himself.

What does this look like practically? This kind of person shows up early and leaves late, displaying the hallmarks of someone who is a good steward of all that's entrusted to them. Christians should be the people who do things before they're asked. We need to take the initiative whenever we become aware of a need or opportunity. I often say, "Find a need and fill it—find a hurt and heal it."

Go the extra mile. Do more than was asked. Give more than is expected. Surprise people with the love of Jesus. This will force people to recognize God's glory and power in your life.

Attitude

Last but not least, the fourth of these key Christlike qualities, symbolized by the ox, points us toward the kind of attitude we must cultivate, one that perseveres and trusts God, steadily walking according to his direction no matter what circumstances may come our way. The ox was known to be a strong, reliable animal that could always be counted on. Similarly, Jesus continued in the work and path God called him to regardless of the judgment and persecution that others threw at him. He was faithful and steady, and because of this, he changed many lives.

We see this attitude on full display in Mark's Gospel, which was written primarily to the Romans to showcase the mighty miracles that Jesus performed. We know that Mark was a disciple of Peter, so Mark's Gospel is primarily Peter's account of Jesus' life. This Gospel brings the total number of Jesus' miracles recorded in all four Gospels to thirty-five. They include:

- 17 bodily cures (leprosy, paralysis, blindness, deaf and dumb, internal hemorrhage, dropsy, fever, etc.)
- 9 miracles over nature (catches of fish, stilling of storms, feeding of multitudes, walking on water, etc.)
- 6 deliverances of demoniacs
- 3 resurrections
- An innumerable multitude of healings for those who simply touched Jesus' garment or those he personally laid hands upon

What do these miracles all have in common besides Jesus' miraculous power? They all show an attitude of calm, resilient unflappability despite what seemed like impossible situations—debilitating sickness, uncontrollable natural circumstances, even the finality of death. With the Holy Spirit living in us, we have the ability to remain faithful, to exude peace, calm, and hope no matter what may happen in our lives. Even in the face of unbearable tragedy and losing loved ones, we know that we can trust God and keep going. We may not know how, but like the ox we can faithfully plod along and know that our burden is light and our yoke is easy.

Paul certainly knew about what it was to remain calm, cool, and collected amid crazy circumstances. When angry leaders told him, "We'll throw you in prison!" Paul almost seemed eager to go back there. We know that while in jail Paul ministered to at least one jailer and finished some of his writings to other believers in other churches (Acts 16:25–31). Remember, he was the disciple of Jesus who considered his life the ultimate win-win situation: If he remained alive on earth, he could tell more people about Christ. If he died and went to heaven, then he would get to be present with the Lord.

We have this same guarantee, and our attitude should reflect it. Are circumstances in your life dragging you down? Are you so overwhelmed by changes in culture that you feel like there's nothing you can do? Then think again, my friend! "You must influence them; do not let them influence you!" (Jer. 15:19 NLT).

It's so important that we examine our lives and surrender our baggage, our worries, our secrets, and our fears all at the foot of the cross. Make a decision to rest in the peace of God no matter your circumstances, to relish this life you've been given. Be a living breath of fresh air wherever you go. This is the essence of faith! Don't bring more problems; bring solutions. Bring a steady certainty of who God is, and allow others to know that he and he alone is the source of your peace and purpose in this life.

The secret of influence isn't what you say; it's how you live.

Jesus is the perfect example of how to engage people's hearts in a shifting culture. Drawing on the four faces of God described in the prophetic books of Ezekiel and Revelation, we find symbols for all the Christlike qualities we need. With the boldness of a lion, we develop courage and character that flows out of real

> The secret of influence isn't what you say; it's how you live.

relationship with our all-powerful, gracious God, drawing other people to him who see this in us and want to know more. With the genuine love for people displayed by the face of the man, we relate to people through humble service, putting their needs above our own. The eagle reminds us to demonstrate a lifestyle that people respect and want, a commitment to excellence second to none. And the ox symbolizes our steady unflappability, despite whatever circumstances may come our way, a real-life manifestation of the peace we find in Jesus.

Like the early believers wanting to change their culture, may we also pray "that this faith we hold in common keeps showing up in the good things we do, and that people recognize Christ in all of it" (Philem. 1:6 MSG). That's the secret to real influence. That's why we've built these four qualities into the culture of our church:

Love God.
Love people.
Do everything with excellence.
Have a good attitude.

It's that simple.

Fifteen

HOW THEN SHALL WE LIVE?

Jesus teaches us another way: Go out. Go out and share your testimony, go out and interact with your brothers, go out and share, go out and ask. Become the Word in body as well as spirit.

—POPE FRANCIS

I hope you haven't started with this chapter.

I've heard some people flip to the last chapter of a book and read it first, and then if they like it, they feel like they've read the whole book. If they don't like it, they believe they've avoided wasting their time. Apparently, some fiction readers want to know how the story ends before they invest any emotional energy in caring for the characters. And certain nonfiction readers want to get the big takeaway points first and then decide if those points are worth a second look.

I have to admit, because I like summaries, lists, and bullet points, this read-the-last-chapter-first logic appeals to me. But I also know that by taking such shortcuts you can miss the entire point of a message. The main reason I hope you haven't started with this chapter is because there are no shortcuts when you try to live out your faith in the context of culture and your everyday life.

I wish there were. In fact, I originally intended to provide you with a series of loose scripts that you could use when you come up against a cultural conflict, an ungodly standard, or a sinful behavior in others. You know, a collection of responses like "What to Say to Your Muslim Coworker" or "How to Talk to Your Gay Nephew" or even "How to Comment on Social Media About Cultural Issues." But if I included those, I would be doing you and those to whom you're relating a grave disservice.

Why? Just think about how annoyed you become when a telemarketer, insurance agent, or customer service rep reads to you from a prescribed script. Those situations are so frustrating because we want to engage in a real conversation with a real human being (or in the case of telemarketers, to be left alone). We need to file a claim or place an order or get an answer to our question, and the person on the other end of the phone can only read (sometimes not so smoothly) a generic response that someone else has written. Not very personal, is it?

It's one thing to deal with this kind of response when you're talking about health deductibles and purchase orders, but when you're trying to connect with someone and share the most important thing in your life with them, it's impossible. I can't tell you the exact words you should say when faced with the cultural challenges in your life. We all have different personalities, relationships, and communication styles. In addition to this, we're all in different places with God in our own seasons of life.

There is no one-size-fits-all for being a Daniel in the culture around you.

The other important reason I hope you're not beginning with this chapter is because there's so much we need to understand before we confront our culture. That's the whole reason I wrote this book! Being a person of godly influence in an ungodly culture requires more than just a personal opinion and a Bible verse. It requires a deep-seated personal faith and intimate relationship with God, along with a reliance on him as your daily power source and guide. In fact, based on what we've seen exemplified by Daniel, here's a short list of what we need to do to get started on being a person of influence in our culture:

- Know our God-given identities (chapter 1)
- Settle our core values (chapter 2)
- Be ready to stand our ground in the tests of life (chapter 3)
- Worship God (chapter 4)
- Don't worship other gods (chapter 5)
- Give our lives fully to Jesus (chapter 6)
- Identify our pride (chapter 7)
- Put our feelings in their proper place (chapter 8)
- Give God full control of our lives (chapter 9)
- Understand the brevity of life (chapter 10)
- Focus on our priorities (chapter 11)
- Heed the warning signs of weariness (chapter 12)
- Learn how to connect before we correct (chapter 13)
- Let God change us into his likeness (chapter 14)

I'm certainly not saying these must be mastered before we can influence others, because none of us have these mastered and never will completely. These elements are progressive in many ways, and we individually may not experience them in this order. But the attitudes and decisions these chapters challenge us to consider need to be in our hearts and minds before we take on the world around us. They equip us in ways that simply can't be attained through any other means. They compel us to grow closer to God and to use this closeness as the motivation for how we stand up in a bow-down world.

As God does a work in us, we become vessels that he can use to impact others. Loved by God, saved by his Son, and empowered by his Spirit, we can influence the culture around us in two major ways: spiritually and relationally. We need first to be prepared spiritually, and then we can engage in cultural relationships with maximum positive impact.

Shining Light in the Darkness

Humans are triune beings: body, soul, and spirit. It's the spirit part of us that is like God and will live forever. And because each and every person has a spirit and is made in the likeness of God, we will always be on a spiritual journey. Like homing pigeons constantly returning to their nests, our spirits are continually in search of their Creator. This innate spiritual part of us explains why we are the only part of creation that worships. And it's also why we need to fight the cultural battle spiritually.

How do we do that? The same way Jesus did. He came face-to-face with the Devil when he was tempted in the wilderness (see Matt. 4 and Luke 4), and every time the Enemy tried to tempt him, Jesus responded with a verse from the Bible. He used the Sword of Truth to defend himself from the Enemy's attacks. Think of it this way: Jesus didn't confront the Devil as God. He confronted the Devil as a man with the Word of God. We should do the same thing.

> Because each and every person has a spirit and is made in the likeness of God, they will always be on a spiritual journey.

Here are five scriptures and five model prayers we can pray (make them your own) for the people God has given us to influence:

1. Pray that the Father would draw them to Jesus.

"No one can come to me unless the Father who sent me draws them" (John 6:44).

I remember the day I gave my life to Jesus. I had been in church my whole life, but this day was different. Something was stirring inside of me. I'm still not sure how best to explain it. I just knew that God was dealing with me, and I needed to respond. There was this natural, magnetic pull to the truth of the gospel—an invisible, irresistible tug on my heart. This is something God does, not something we can make happen out of our own strivings, so we need to be faithful in praying that the Father would draw those he's placed on our hearts to Jesus.

> Father, I pray for the people around me, that you would supernaturally draw their hearts to you. Send your Holy Spirit to them, and give them the desire to give their lives to you. Help them to recognize their longing for more as spiritual, as a thirst only you can quench. Open their ears to hear your voice.

2. Bind the spirit that blinds their minds.

"The god of this age has blinded the minds of unbelievers, so that they cannot see the light of the gospel that displays the glory of Christ, who is the image of God" (2 Cor. 4:4).

The truth can be right in front of some people, and they still can't see it. That's because something is in the way. Something is blocking their view of God. We can pray against whatever is in the way, though, so they can see the light of God. We can pray that they would see the truth without any obstacles or distractions interfering.

> Father, bind the evil spirits that are blinding the minds of the people around me in the name of Jesus. I pray that they would be able to see clearly, to recognize who you are, and to give their hearts to you. Remove all hindrances

the Enemy would use to distract them from your truth. Open their eyes, Lord, that they might see Jesus.

3. Let loose the spirit of adoption (personal relationship with God).

"The Spirit you received does not make you slaves, so that you live in fear again; rather, the Spirit you received brought about your adoption to sonship. And by him we cry, 'Abba, Father'" (Rom. 8:15).

Many people think Christianity is just another religion. They only see God through the lens of the organization and institution of the church. They may even feel frustrated, angry, or betrayed by people in churches they have encountered or by religious legalists and their hypocrisy. But God didn't come to build an organization. He came to have relationship with his children. He wants his kids to come home. Praying for people to have personal encounters with the living God makes a huge difference.

> Father, I pray that people will understand how much you love them. Loose the spirit of adoption for the people around me, so that they come into a meaningful relationship with you. Stir in their hearts a longing to come home, to hear your voice, and to see you welcoming them with open arms. Let them know you are always running to meet them and hold them close.

4. Pray that believers will enter into positive relationships with the lost, and pray that we will see the opportunities that come across our paths.

"Ask the Lord of the harvest, therefore, to send out workers into his harvest field" (Matt. 9:38).

This one is twofold: we can pray for other Christians to

influence the people around them positively, and we can also look for opportunities to influence others positively ourselves. God's plan to reach people is worked through those who already know and love him. Jesus asked us to pray for people to go into the world and be salt and light. He came to bring the good news of the gospel to all people, and his desire is that everyone would know and love him. As his "spiritual farmers," we should be attuned to opportunities to plant spiritual seeds in the lives of the people we encounter each day. We may have no idea who has already been praying for them and the culminating impact a kind word, a compassionate act, or a loving attitude can have to draw someone to Christ.

> Father, I pray for the lost around me to meet believers who will influence them in a positive way. Lord, let my life shine in such a way that people want to know the God I serve. Allow others to see my genuine love and concern for them in all that I say and do. Let me be your hands and feet to serve them and let them know just how much you love them.

5. Release the spirit of wisdom and revelation on them, so they may know God better.

"I keep asking that the God of our Lord Jesus Christ, the glorious Father, may give you the Spirit of wisdom and revelation, so that you may know him better" (Eph. 1:17).

It's that "eureka" moment. That "aha!" when it finally clicks. It happens in class when you suddenly understand the math equation or how something works. The most important moment for it to happen is when the lights come on spiritually. People need to see their own sin, see what Jesus did on the cross, and see the hope that comes from giving their life to God. They need wisdom, not just knowledge, of spiritual things and insight into how spiritual things directly impact them.

> Father, I pray for the people around me to experience the spirit of wisdom and revelation. I pray that they would truly understand their spiritual condition and see what Jesus did for them on the cross. Help them to have the information and experiences needed to come to you, so they can understand all you have for them.

Confronting Cultural Challenges

Once the spiritual groundwork has been laid, we can work on being Christ's ambassadors in the world around us. As I promised you earlier, there are no set scripts, shortcuts, or easy answers here. It takes time to lay the spiritual groundwork and to invest in relationships. There's no magic formula.

However, I do have suggestions. Below are five approaches or attitudes of response you can incorporate as you engage with the people God has given you to influence. Because I'm frequently asked how I handle certain situations, I'm including a very basic conversational response, based on my past experience, for you to use mostly as a prompt to get started on each of the five. Again, you don't need to memorize these or say them verbatim when talking to someone about cultural challenges. Just keep it real, and let God's Holy Spirit give you wisdom and discernment about how to respond and what to say.

1. Keep your standards high and your grace deep.

> For the message of the cross is foolishness to those who are perishing, but to us who are being saved it is the power of God. For it is written:

"I will destroy the wisdom of the wise;
    the intelligence of the intelligent I will frustrate."
Where is the wise person? Where is the teacher of the law?
Where is the philosopher of this age? Has not God made foolish
the wisdom of the world? (1 Cor. 1:18–20)

The apostle Paul wrote this letter to the church in Corinth to deal with how culture was affecting their church. He encouraged the followers of Jesus there to keep the standards high but in a grace-filled way. He pointed out that those who think they are smarter than God will discover their own limits and end up frustrated. To illustrate this, Paul asked several rhetorical questions: "Where's the smarty pants who thinks they know so much? Where's the wise guy or the know-it-all? Where's the 'enlightened expert' of the times? Hasn't God shown you all how silly your views are compared to his?" Obviously, this is my paraphrase, but I think you get the point of what Paul was saying. He concluded, "For the foolishness of God is wiser than human wisdom, and the weakness of God is stronger than human strength" (1 Cor. 1:25).

Throughout the rest of his letter, which we know as 1 Corinthians, Paul confronted culture and culture's norms but managed to do so with grace. He clearly took a strong stand against sinful behavior and immoral standards and practices, but the way he did it displays compassion and not condemnation, heartfelt concern and not self-righteous indignation.

Similarly, we need to think less about who we might offend and, with grace and truth, take a stand for God's Word. I suspect many of us don't like dealing with this culture clash between the world's ways and God's ways. We often want the world to like us more than we want to stand strong for God's ways. The reality is that the world is going to think God's ways and standards are foolish. They are going to want us to change what we believe.

So here's the real question: What are we going to do when we face this dilemma? What's our response going to be when confronted with a clash between the culture around us and the God we love and want to serve?

We should do as Jesus did and keep the standards high and the grace deep. Everyone in Jesus' day knew the Ten Commandments and that adultery was wrong, but then Jesus came along and said, "If you've ever even looked at another person and lusted, you've committed adultery in your heart" (Matt. 5:28, my paraphrase). In one sentence, Jesus made an adulterer of almost everyone in the audience! Jesus didn't lower the standard. He pointed toward a higher standard, and then he refused to condemn those who fell short of it.

> We should do as Jesus did and keep the standards high and the grace deep.

In other words, he didn't cave to the cultural pressure so that he could be liked and accepted. Jesus didn't say what people wanted to hear or what would make them feel good. He pointed to a higher standard and then provided a way out for those who would repent. See the difference? The standard got *higher*, but the grace got *deeper*.

This is how we should engage the culture and its standards. Let's stick to God's way and God's Word. If the Bible calls it sin, then it's sin—period. Let's not give into the pressure to change because the world thinks it's foolish. God's ways will always be foolish to the world. Instead, let's point to a higher standard but extend the deep, abundant grace that we all need.

When faced with a discussion about any moral issue, I often say something like this:

We all fall short of God's standards—you, me, everybody. But let's not change his truth to fit what we want. Let's ask God to change us to fit what he wants. That's why he's God and we're his creation. He knows what's best for us and loves us enough to tell us those boundaries. Moral standards aren't manmade; they're God-given.

2. Accept people without approving of their behavior.

"But Daniel resolved not to defile himself with the royal food and wine, and he asked the chief official for permission not to defile himself this way" (Dan. 1:8).

Jesus confronted the culture around him all the time. Remember the scene found in John 8, where a woman was caught in adultery by the religious leaders and Pharisees? They brought her before Jesus, who had been teaching in the temple courts, in hopes of tripping him up. They reminded Jesus that the law under Moses required that anyone caught in adultery be stoned. These leaders plotting against Jesus hoped that he would either refute the law of Moses or else indirectly endorse killing the woman standing before them in the midst of a large crowd.

Jesus didn't fall for it, however. We're told that Jesus began writing something in the dusty ground with his finger. When the religious leaders kept goading him, Jesus said, "Let any one of you who is without sin be the first to throw a stone at her" (John 8:7). Then he started writing in the dust again as the Pharisees and other religious leaders walked away.

While we're not told what Jesus wrote, it wouldn't surprise me if it was a list of the specific sins each of the religious leaders had committed. Maybe it was something else, but whatever it was, the message was clear. When Jesus asked who was left to accuse her, the woman told him none remained. He replied, "Then neither do I condemn you. . . . Go now and leave your life of sin" (John 8:11).

Jesus masterfully accepted and respected her without approving of her behavior. He showed compassion rather than join in with her accusers. He gave her a hopeful doorway out of her sinful life. There's no better model for how we engage those around us who are participating in behaviors God identifies as sinful.

When faced with someone I know and care about who is living in direct contrast to the ways of God, I usually try to express something like this:

God loves us just the way we are, but too much to let us stay that way. He doesn't condemn us, but he does want to change us. I think it's similar to how I feel about my children. I try to love each one uniquely and unconditionally. But I still want them to do what's truly best for them—not just whatever they feel like doing.

3. *Never let the tone get contentious.*

"When Arioch, the commander of the king's guard, had gone out to put to death the wise men of Babylon, Daniel spoke to him with wisdom and tact" (Dan. 2:14).

The irony of this approach is that our culture loves to encourage and exploit contentiousness. For many people, businesses, and organizations, any time spent in the spotlight of public attention—no matter how controversial the catalyst—is valuable. Social media and our Internet-driven culture reinforce the belief that everyone's opinions, on all topics and at all times, not only matter but must be shared. And as we've all learned by now, plenty of mean-spirited critics and "haters" thrive online just by ranting and raving.

Perhaps it's even worse when a personal conversation becomes contentious, with each party suddenly becoming defensive or even angry and antagonistic. However, the moment that dynamic surfaces, the opportunity for any real communication has pretty much disappeared. Whenever a friendly, respectful discussion becomes a political debate, power struggle, or theological boxing match, it feels like a personal attack. Everyone quits listening at that point and either runs for cover, retreating and withdrawing, or prepares to fight, looking for points of attack.

The examples set by Daniel and Jesus are clear, not to mention numerous others including Paul and James: our words matter because they reveal our hearts. Here's what Jesus himself had to say about the power of our words to reveal what's inside us:

> For the mouth speaks what the heart is full of. A good man brings good things out of the good stored up in him, and an evil man brings evil things out of the evil stored up in him. But I tell you that everyone will have to give account on the day of judgment for every empty word they have spoken. For by your words you will be acquitted, and by your words you will be condemned. (Matt. 12:34–37)

The moment you make engaging with other people about "being right," you need to stop and check your heart. You may need to apologize, share what you're feeling, or leave and try again another day. But arguing with someone, let alone condemning them and their behavior as sinful, has never won a single person to the Lord. Even if they don't show it or you can't see it, most people already feel the weight of their secrets, their sins, and their struggles. They don't need someone pressing down and adding to that weight. They need hope. They need someone who says, "I know what that feels like, but now I know the freedom of being forgiven."

If you struggle with letting your emotions get out of hand

> The moment you make engaging with other people about "being right," you need to stop and check your heart.

when relating to nonbelievers, then the best remedy I know is spending time with God. His heart always replenishes our experience of grace. When we encounter his mercy, love, and forgiveness, it's hard not to pass it on to those around us.

Whenever I find myself in a cultural conversation that heats up, I usually try to change the tone of our discussion by saying:

> Hey, I can tell we're both passionate about our beliefs. But I don't want to argue about this. I'd rather have a relationship with you than win an argument. We can come back to this another time—tell me about . . . [your pet, your kids, your job, whatever will change the topic and build a relational bridge].

4. Lead them to truth by identifying with their struggle.

"And you must show mercy to those whose faith is wavering. Rescue others by snatching them from the flames of judgment. Show mercy to still others, but do so with great caution, hating the sins that contaminate their lives" (Jude vv. 22–23 NLT).

We should never shame or condemn people for their feelings—including same-sex attraction or desires to do immoral things. Why? Because we all have feelings, and just because we feel a certain way doesn't mean we have to act on those feelings.

I have my own set of desires outside of God's standard. In fact, I'm aware of it every time I read Scripture. As I have said, I'm not predisposed to monogamy. If a beautiful woman walks by, my flesh wants to lust. When this happens, I don't just accept my lustful feelings; instead, I identify them as wrong, repent, and thank God for his grace and ask him to do a work inside of me. And we do the same thing for anyone who is struggling with anything. We embrace them as long as they desire repentance.

If they don't desire repentance and want you to approve of their sin, then, obviously, that's something you cannot do.

However, withholding your approval does not mean condemning them. Too often, our culture likes to go to extremes—either we're in full agreement or else we're totally opposed. This kind of attitude makes it even more difficult for us as Christians to accept others without approving of their sinful standards or behaviors.

One way to live within this tension, however, is by identifying with their struggle. Other people are turned off when we come across—even unintentionally—as better than them, self-righteous, or legalistic. Nothing turns me off like a smug attitude, no matter the situation. When we display humility, authenticity, honesty, or even humor when appropriate, we relate to others as human beings, person to person, and eventually, heart to heart.

Once that heart connection takes place, you'll find people are much more willing to hear the truth. When they know you and trust you and see that you're for real, then they want to have what you have. They want to know Jesus.

When people defend their actions based on their feelings, I try to identify with the struggle our feelings can cause:

> You know, I struggle too. My feelings sometimes get in the way of the kind of person I want to be, the kind of person God wants me to be. I often desire things outside of God's will for my life. While I've learned we can't always change our feelings, we can evaluate them, see where they're leading us, and ask God to change us.

5. Paint the picture of what it looks like to come home.

"But while he was still a long way off, his father saw him and was filled with compassion for him; he ran to his son, threw his arms around him and kissed him" (Luke 15:20).

No matter what someone has done or not done, it's never too late for God to forgive them and to transform their lives. Our job is to make sure they know this, to paint an accurate and vivid picture of what it's like to come home to the Lord. There are numerous ways to do this, especially once you know a person and have developed a level of trust or a heart connection with them.

Look for opportunities to build bridges and care for people every chance you get. This is the example we see throughout Jesus' life. When he saw someone's need, he met it—and then he addressed the greater spiritual need. Let those around you know you're always willing and available to listen, to talk, even to pray with them. You'd be surprised how many non-Christians will ask me to pray with them. The goal is to always show a welcoming spirit of kindness, generosity, and graciousness. Leave the porch light on for them. This gives them a strong sense of the safe place that is coming home to God.

> Look for opportunities to build bridges and care for people every chance you get.

When people reject God's way, sometimes the best thing to do is wait and let them realize for themselves that going their own way doesn't work. When they choose their own direction, I usually say something like:

If you ever change your mind—if you ever decide that your way isn't working—if you ever find yourself in a miserable place and want to come home, I want to be the first person you call. I'm always willing to listen and help however I can.

Be the Daniel of Your Day

Let me be honest with you. If you're willing to adopt these five approaches, you will still struggle at times with what to say or how to respond to those around you. You might still have a hard time not letting your emotions erupt when confronted with culture's sinful standards. You may even find yourself more aware of and more sensitively attuned to the clash between God's ways and the ways of the world. But the key is to not give up.

As we saw time and time again, Daniel stood his ground—even risking his life—to oppose the cultural pressure surrounding him. He didn't argue, defend, explain, or debate. He simply made his boundaries clear with direct, respectful communication. As a result, Daniel shone like a beacon of God's truth for seventy years, valued and esteemed by four different Babylonian regimes.

When culture shifts—and we know it always will—we should get excited. Because in the midst of those chaotic, unsettling changes, we live on solid ground. In Christ we have the hope the world needs. And like the prophet Daniel, we are catalysts for redemptive change, people of influence who know our goal is not to be right but to be *effective*. People willing to stand when it's easier to bow under the weight of culture. People whose light shines brighter in the darkness of a sinful culture.

The world is waiting on what you have to offer! Let them see Christ in you. Let all that you do be done in love.

CONCLUSION
When Is Jesus Coming Back?

Eternity is really long, especially near the end.

—WOODY ALLEN

Most of these pages you've just read were inspired by and based on the first half of the book of Daniel. It has all the cool stories we usually associate with him—the Daniel "diet," the fiery furnace, the lions' den. These stories all reveal Daniel's key point, which is the same one I've tried to make throughout this book: when faced with cultural pressure, don't compromise your faith or the opportunity to influence the world for God's kingdom.

The entire nation of Israel was held captive in Babylon, and although they wanted to live and serve the true living God, the culture around them demanded something else. As I shared at the beginning of this journey, I can think of no better field guide for us today than the example set by Daniel more than two thousand years ago. Our culture is sliding, shifting, slipping away before our eyes each day. What can we do about it?

If you've read this far, then you clearly want to do something, to stand your ground and, like Daniel, to be a person of influence in the culture around you. While I've done my best to equip you, based on the first half of Daniel's writings along with other Scripture, I would be doing you an injustice if I didn't share at least a little about the message found in the second half of Daniel.

Signs of the Time

When I'm talking with other people about how to remain godly in an ungodly culture, there's often a natural progression to discussing end times. With all the immoral, chaotic, never-seen-before depravity in the world around us, it's logical to think we must be getting close to the end of time, to the day when Jesus will return to earth. This concern is nothing new and has fascinated, terrified, and motivated people from the moment Jesus ascended until today. I can assure you that we're not going to know exactly when he will return. In fact, Jesus himself said as much: "But about that day or hour no one knows, not even the angels in heaven, nor the Son, but only the Father" (Matt. 24:36).

> When faced with cultural pressure, don't compromise your faith or the opportunity to influence the world for God's kingdom.

Jesus understood, then as now, that people want a specific, concrete answer to this question. They want charts and graphs and timelines and boxes that can be checked off a list. But he made it clear that wasn't going to happen and that it wasn't even possible, because even he didn't know—only his Father knows. Jesus' followers finally wised up a little bit and asked a different, albeit related, question: "As Jesus was sitting on the Mount of Olives, the disciples came to him privately. 'Tell us,' they said, 'when will this happen, and what will be the sign of your coming and of the end of the age?'" (Matt. 24:3).

Jesus answered their question with a list of signs and indications of his imminent return. He then concluded:

> Because of the increase of wickedness, the love of most will grow cold, but the one who stands firm to the end will be saved. And

251

this gospel of the kingdom will be preached in the whole world as
a testimony to all nations, and then the end will come.

So when you see standing in the holy place "the abomination
that causes desolation," spoken of through the prophet Daniel—
let the reader understand." (Matt. 24:12–15)

See the connection? Here we see Jesus himself validate Daniel
as a prophetic book. He basically says that the events Daniel saw
and prophesied are still to come. Notice the general requisites he
mentions: the increase of wickedness, the falling away of many
and the steadfastness of only a few, and the way the gospel will be
preached throughout the world.

If you need further evidence of Daniel's prophetic relevance to
the end times, just consider this: Daniel is the most quoted source
in Revelation. While numerous books of the Old Testament are
referenced in Revelation, Daniel comes up more than thirty times.
Daniel definitely knew something about Christ's return.

Of the dozen chapters in Daniel, six of them reveal a series
of prophetic dreams and visions he had. While they all reveal the
future, and while Jesus reinforced their ongoing relevancy for us
today, everyone does not agree on how we should interpret them.
In case you haven't noticed, there are as many different theological perspectives on eschatology, or how to study end times, as
there are churches around the world. They range from being his-
toric pre-millennialist to dispensational post-millennialist. You
might even be an All-American amillennialist or a super-duper
supersessionist. Or, like many people, you could be a plain old
pan-millennialist—someone who believes it's all going to pan out
in the end!

Regardless of your views about how and when it's all going
to end, we can all agree that we need to regard it with wisdom. I
don't claim to have all the answers or the perfect interpretation of

prophecy from the Bible. But I do want to share briefly with you what I see there, specifically in Daniel and the way Daniel is cross-referenced in Revelation. As we wrap up our time together, I want to dip into the last half of Daniel, connect it to Revelation, and tell you what I think it means for us today. I encourage you to study these passages in more depth and to forgive me for distilling them down to what I see as their essence. Consider my final thoughts here as a kind of exclamation point to the rest of this book.

Because no matter when Jesus comes back, we all need to be ready.

Multiplication Test

Like many of the Old Testament prophets, Daniel foretold the coming of the Messiah, the one God would someday send to rescue his people from their sins. In the second half of the book of Daniel, there's one place where Daniel summarizes all his prophetic visions and explains them by way of what he calls the "seventy sevens." The word for "seventy" is straightforward and means the number 70. The word for "sevens," however, comes from the Hebrew word *shavuah*, which literally means a period of time based on seven increments.

Originally, some Bible translators thought this word meant "week," which seems logical because in our way of keeping time, seven days make a week. However, taken in context of history, it's clear Daniel is describing periods of seven *years*. So, his summary of what he's seen regarding the future comes down to viewing it in seventy different seven-year periods. Using our multiplication skills, we see that Daniel prophetically revealed 490 (70 x 7) years of future events. Here's how he described these "70 sevens":

Seventy "sevens" are decreed for your people and your holy city to finish transgression, to put an end to sin, to atone for wickedness, to bring in everlasting righteousness, to seal up vision and prophecy and to anoint the Most Holy Place.

Know and understand this: From the time the word goes out to restore and rebuild Jerusalem until the Anointed One, the ruler, comes, there will be seven "sevens," and sixty-two "sevens." It will be rebuilt with streets and a trench, but in times of trouble. After the sixty-two "sevens," the Anointed One will be put to death and will have nothing. The people of the ruler who will come will destroy the city and the sanctuary. The end will come like a flood: War will continue until the end, and desolations have been decreed. He will confirm a covenant with many for one "seven." In the middle of the "seven" he will put an end to sacrifice and offering. And at the temple he will set up an abomination that causes desolation, until the end that is decreed is poured out on him. (Dan. 9:24–27)

Now, what's interesting about Daniel's list of signs is that all of them have been fulfilled in different generations. No wonder, then, that almost every generation thought they were the generation that would see the return of Christ. Probably one of the best guesses would have been during World War II, when the countries around the globe obviously faced wars and rumors of wars. Add in a figure like Hitler, and many people logically thought, *Wow, he's got to be the anti-Christ.* However, looking back now, we know that despite the fulfillment of all these signs, we're still waiting. And here's why: while multiple generations have experienced various signs, no one generation has experienced them all at the same time.

Until now. Our generation is the first one in which this is the case. You and I are alive during a time when all the biblical, prophetic signs are being fulfilled at the same time. This is my basis for believing we are not only in the end times, but we are at the end of the end times.

Here's how I summarize this key passage: Daniel saw 70 seven-year periods, a total of 490 years, of prophecy. Of this total, 69 of those 70 seven-year periods have been fulfilled. In other words, 483 of the 490 years of future events Daniel saw in his visions have already transpired. Only the last seven-year period remains.

By the way, all the things Daniel prophesied about in those first 483 years? All true. For example, he predicted Alexander the Great. Daniel could foresee a king coming from the Greeks. He saw the Roman Empire taken over. He described it all years before-hand, and it all played out exactly like he saw it. I could write an entire book—and some people have—on the ways Daniel's prophecies have been fulfilled. But for our purposes, I just want to briefly spotlight my view on the last seven-year period, namely, that we are already on the cusp of it.

While I don't think we have entered into this last seven-year period, I do believe it's imminent. Why? Because the requisite prophecies have been fulfilled and the world stage has been set for Jesus' return. Daniel talked about it, Jesus talked about it, Paul talked about it, Peter talked about it, and, of course, the entire book of Revelation focuses on John's vision of those last seven years of tribulation. I'm convinced we have reached the beginning of the end.

To Infinity and Beyond

Even if you disagree with me, which I certainly respect your right to do, I hope you will agree that with each flip of the calendar, each digital blink of the clock, all of us are one day closer to Christ's return. Whenever people ask me, "Are we living in the end times?

Are these the last days?" I always tell them, "Yes, these are definitely your last days!" It goes back to the message that mysterious hand wrote on the Babylonian king's wall that Daniel had to decipher: Our days are numbered. Our time is short. We're told:

> But the day of the Lord will come like a thief. The heavens will disappear with a roar; the elements will be destroyed by fire, and the earth and everything done in it will be laid bare.
>
> Since everything will be destroyed in this way, what kind of people ought you to be? You ought to live holy and godly lives as you look forward to the day of God and speed its coming. (2 Peter 3:10–12)

Once again, we're reminded that we're not able to predict the exact time of Christ's return. If you could predict when a thief was going to break into your house, you would call the police or you might just stay up with a gun in hand. You would be ready. But since we're not able to know the time, we can quit worrying and putting our energy into figuring it out. Instead, we should focus on answering a different, more urgent question: "What kind of people ought you to be?"

If we want to stand strong in a bow-down culture, we need to be ready for Christ's return.

We need to be ready. I personally believe we are the generation that is seeing the fulfillment of all the signs. Because it's going to happen as unexpectedly as a thief in the night, we need to be ready. Ask yourself every day, "What kind of person should I be, knowing I am living in an age that could be the end times?"

This passage from 2 Peter answers our question: "You need to live holy and godly." Here *holy* doesn't mean perfect; it means separate. It's *hagios* in the Greek, and it literally means "just don't be all up in that junk." We've got to be in the world without being of the world. We've got to be in culture without culture permeating us. We've got to influence the culture, not reflect the culture.

After we're told to live holy and separate lives, in the world but not of it, notice the last phrase: ". . . and you can actually speed the return of Christ" (2 Peter 3:12, my paraphrase). *Really?* Did you know that you play a role in the return of Christ? Daniel confirms this as well: "Those who are wise will shine like the brightness of the heavens, and those who lead many to righteousness, like the stars for ever and ever" (Dan. 12:3).

> We've got to influence the culture, not reflect the culture.

Could it be any clearer? *Go, be a shining light, lead many to righteousness.* When we do, we aid and assist in the return of Christ himself on the earth. That's why we need to come together and be a church that is on mission to reach as many people as we possibly can. That's what God is asking us to do.

If we don't want to compromise our faith but we do want to influence our culture, then we must follow God first.

Culture changes; God doesn't. We need to follow him, not culture. As we see on a daily basis, culture is constantly changing. The crucial question becomes, *are we going to change with it?* If we change with it, we are not part of the wise. We're part of the group that just got duped, enamored with all its stuff. We've got to let the Word of God be our standard and then follow him, not the clamor of voices yelling from every direction around us.

We must reject the deception and moral corruption all around us without giving up on other people. In our influence, we are to be a part of the world. In our hearts, we are to be separate. Here's how Paul expressed this tension: "May your whole spirit, soul and body be kept blameless at the coming of our Lord Jesus Christ" (1 Thess. 5:23).

Finally, if we want to live a godly life in an ungodly culture, we must make the most of the life and resources we've been given.

In all places, at all times, preach the gospel with your attitude and actions. And if you need to use words, do that too.

Don't lose your focus on what this life is really all about. Remember: "Be very careful, then, how you live—not as unwise but as wise, making the most of every opportunity, because the days are evil. Therefore do not be foolish, but understand what the Lord's will is" (Eph. 5:15–17). Find your God-given purpose, his will for your life, and make the most of it. Daniel was a prisoner of war, a teenager enslaved by people with customs and values almost the exact opposite of his own. And yet, he still found a way to be the person God created him to be: a prophet, a spokesman of truth, a shining example to people everywhere. Even now, thousands of years later, we see the impact a person of influence can exert.

Do whatever it takes—short of sin—to bring as many people as you can with you into heaven. Don't resign yourself to defeat when you read headlines or confront the sinful behavior of others. Don't compromise your values and think there's nothing you can do. Don't give up on people just because they disagree with you. You have a glorious hope, the only real hope, to offer others. Make the most of your life, even though these days are evil, and make the most of this opportunity that God has given you. He's strategically placed you in the most important generation of all times. Don't waste it.

Your time to shine is now!

ACKNOWLEDGMENTS

There are always more people involved in a project than everyone sees. I am grateful to all the "unseen" people who offered support, encouragement, and assistance with this book. I could not do it without you all.

First, I want to acknowledge and thank Tammy, my incredible wife, for encouraging me to write. I could not do what I do without your love and support.

I want to thank John Maxwell for helping me see how critical it is to stand firm and love well. You embody this message like no other person I know.

Thanks to my fantastic writer, Dudley Delffs, for being a part of my life and ministry. You captured my heart and soul for this project and put it on the page like no other.

A big thank-you to my agent, Matt Yates. You have been there through the whole process and have added so much more than I could have done on my own.

A huge thank-you to Lysa TerKeurst and the team at Proverbs 31. Who knew when my son married your daughter that I would get more than a family member? You are one of the most brilliant writers I know. Thank you so much for helping me with this project.

Special thanks to the team at Thomas Nelson. Your professionalism and passion have been a joy. And a special shout-out to my editor, Jessica Wong, for making this book so much better. Thank you for partnering with me.

I am so grateful for my staff and the congregation at Church of the Highlands. Teaching these principles to you is what inspired me to share it with others. I love being your pastor.

Special thanks to Karol Hobbs, my executive assistant. You pour yourself into everything I do and add so much value to me every day. Thank you.

And of course, all thanks to the only One who is worthy of praise, Jesus Christ my Lord. It is my honor to serve you.

NOTES

Chapter 2: The Strategy to Tame Me

1. Barna Research Group, "Americans Are Most Likely to Base Truth on Feelings," Barna.com, February 12, 2002, https://barna.org /component/content/article/5-barna-update/45-barna-update-sp -657/67-americans-are-most-likely-to-base-truth-on-feelings# .V2f1r03mrDc.
2. Ibid.
3. Ibid.

Chapter 4: When They Say I Must

1. Alison Flood, "Fifty Shades of Grey Sequel Breaks Sales Records," *Guardian*, June 2, 2015, https://www.theguardian.com/books/2015 /jun/23/fifty-shades-of-grey-sequel-breaks-sales-records.

Chapter 5: When They Say I Can't

1. David Barton, *America: To Pray or Not to Pray* (Houston: Wallbuilders Press, 1997), 97–105.
2. Ibid.

3. Ryan T. Anderson, "In NM, Same-Sex Marriage Trumps Religious Liberty," *Christian Post*, August 26, 2013, http://www.christianpost. com/news/in-nm-same-sex-marriage-trumps-religious-liberty -103024/#A4c5p7w8k7VXhF3K.99\.

Chapter 7: End-Times Insanity

1. Jack Hyles, "Exploring Prayer with Jack Hyles," Jack Hyles Home Page, accessed July 7, 2017, www.jackhyles.com/exploringprayer.

Chapter 8: The Art of Dying

1. George Barna, *Third Millennium Teens* (Ventura: Barna Research, 2000), 56–57.

Chapter 9: It's a Control Issue

1. Martin Luther King, Jr., in a speech aired February 27, 1967, in San Francisco. KPIX Eyewitness News, "Dr. Martin Luther King, Jr. on Racial Segregation" (video), San Francisco Bay Area Television Archive, updated October 22, 2011, https://diva.sfsu.edu/collections /sfbatv/bundles/190080.

About the Author

C hris Hodges, founding and senior pastor of Church of the Highlands, is known for his relevant teaching style and his passion for raising up global leaders to fulfill the Great Commission. Chris and his wife, Tammy, have five children and live in Birmingham, Alabama, where Church of the Highlands began in 2001.

Providing life-giving community focused on the simplicity of the gospel along with the power of an intimate relationship with a loving God, Chris continues changing the way church is done worldwide. Under his leadership, Church of the Highlands has launched campuses all across the state of Alabama and has grown to more than forty-five thousand people attending weekly.

Outreach magazine recently ranked Highlands as the second-largest evangelical church in America, and the sixth-fastest in growth. Highlands remains completely debt-free and operates on a budget less than 70 percent of the income of the church. With this margin, Highlands builds all new facilities with cash and gives more than $10 million per year to missions and church planting.

Chris cofounded the Association of Related Churches (ARC

at arcchurches.com) in 2001, which trains more than one thousand church planters every year and gives more than $4 million annually to church planters. To date, ARC has planted more than 630 churches across the USA (now averaging more than one hundred new churches every year).

Chris also founded a coaching network called GROW (growleader.com) to help churches reach their full growth potential. Each year more than four thousand pastors attend sold-out conferences and roundtables in America and Europe led by Chris, his team, and special guests. These events train pastors and leaders in a simple yet systematic model based on his bestselling books *Four Cups* and *Fresh Air*. Thousands of churches now use his model and continue breaking growth barriers.

As chancellor of Highlands College (thehighlandscollege .com), a two-year ministry training college that gives students a chance to receive hands-on ministry training in a healthy college environment, Chris emphasizes relationships and spiritual growth as top priorities. Students are currently being developed in areas such as Ministry Leadership, Worship, and Creative Arts.

Chris regularly speaks at strategic conferences and groundbreaking churches, including:

- Hillsong Conference and Hillsong
  Church (Pastor Brian Houston)
- EQUIP, a global leadership training organization
  founded by John Maxwell for which Chris
  serves on the board of directors
- Gateway Church and Gateway Conference
  (Pastor Robert Morris)

Chris's educational background includes a BA in management from Colorado Christian University and a Masters of Ministry from Southwestern Christian University.